IMAGES
of America

WILTON

IN THE GOLDEN AGE OF POSTCARDS

IMAGES
of America

WILTON

IN THE GOLDEN AGE OF POSTCARDS

Laurie J. Bepler and Virginia B. Bepler

ARCADIA
PUBLISHING

ISBN 978-0-7385-9032-5

Published by Arcadia Publishing
Charleston, South Carolina

Printed in the United States of America

For all general information contact Arcadia Publishing at:
Telephone 843-853-2070
Fax 843-853-0044
E-mail sales@arcadiapublishing.com
For customer service and orders:
Toll-Free 1-888-313-2665

Visit us on the Internet at www.arcadiapublishing.com

Contents

Introduction 7

1. Early Wilton Postcards 9
2. Mixed Methods 25
3. Mixed Methods: Local and National 43
4. Commercialism Comes to Wilton 61
5. Wilton Joins the World 75
6. Old Friends and Neighbors 87

List of References 95

Acknowledgments 96

Dedicated to the Bradleys and Beplers,

who ensured our memories.

Introduction

Wilton is one of the daughter towns of Norwalk. Her children settled along the Norwalk River valley and established a town center before spreading out into the hills. By 1802 the town was incorporated and had developed mills, churches, and schools. By the late 1800s, when the postcard became an easy communication tool, Wilton also had post offices and a railroad.

The postcard, or the penny postcard, as it was familiarly known, was an economical way to send a brief message. The first postcards were made in Austria in 1869, and other nations soon followed suit. The cards have evolved from those designed for messages only (private mailing cards) to cards containing an address and postage on one side and picture and message on the other (such cards are called undivided backs). Since 1907, the new, more familiar "divided backs" have been used.

The sensitive, postcard-sized photographic paper produced by Kodak and other vendors was a great aid to early local photographers and made possible many small-town scenes from the early 1900s. Various publishing companies would photograph a group of local views and sell them to an outlet in the area.

Wilton's postcards may be categorized by publisher and date. Although many early postcards were photographed and published in America, they were actually printed in Germany, where a technically superior process had been developed before World War I. It is interesting to note in Wilton's cards the trends that existed in the business as a whole.

In creating this book, we have been putting together memories. It has become important to research all the postcards that have been made of Wilton subjects. Certain sites appear over and over. These are the important memories of Wilton, the images we should not lose sight of in the modern, technological world. Let us remember the classical architecture of old homes and public buildings, the waterways, and the simple schools that have led the way to higher education.

By keeping these memories in visible form, we come to know the whole spirit of Wilton.

V.B.B.

One

Early Wilton Postcards

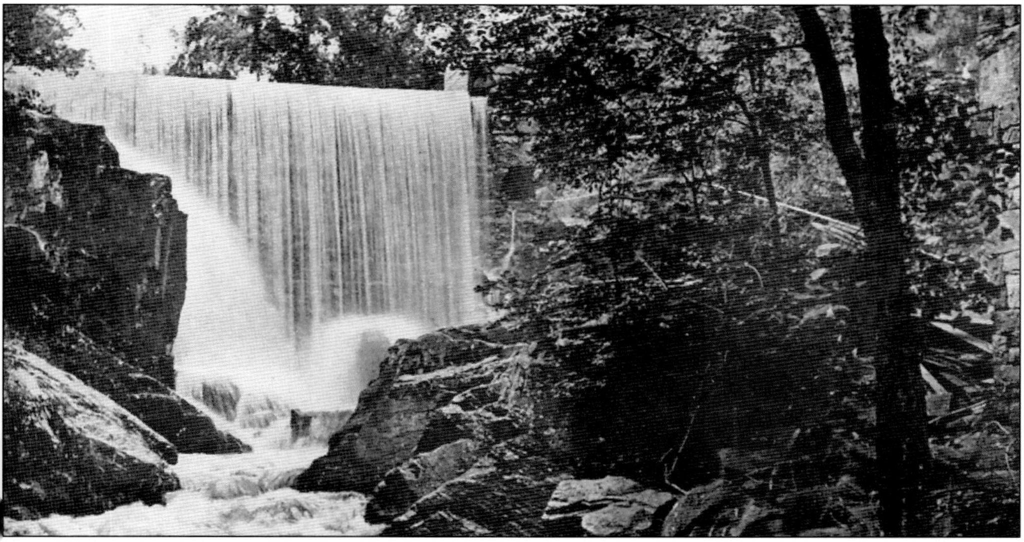

These cards, apparently locally photographed and published, use the undivided backs that the government allowed before 1907. The numbered cards must have been part of a set of about twenty. The total set has not been found.

There have been mills on this stream since about 1725. The west branch of the Norwalk River, also called the Comstock Brook, has fueled industries that provided the sawing, grinding, and fulling of cloth. Several generations of Olmsteads and Merwins have been associated with this area.

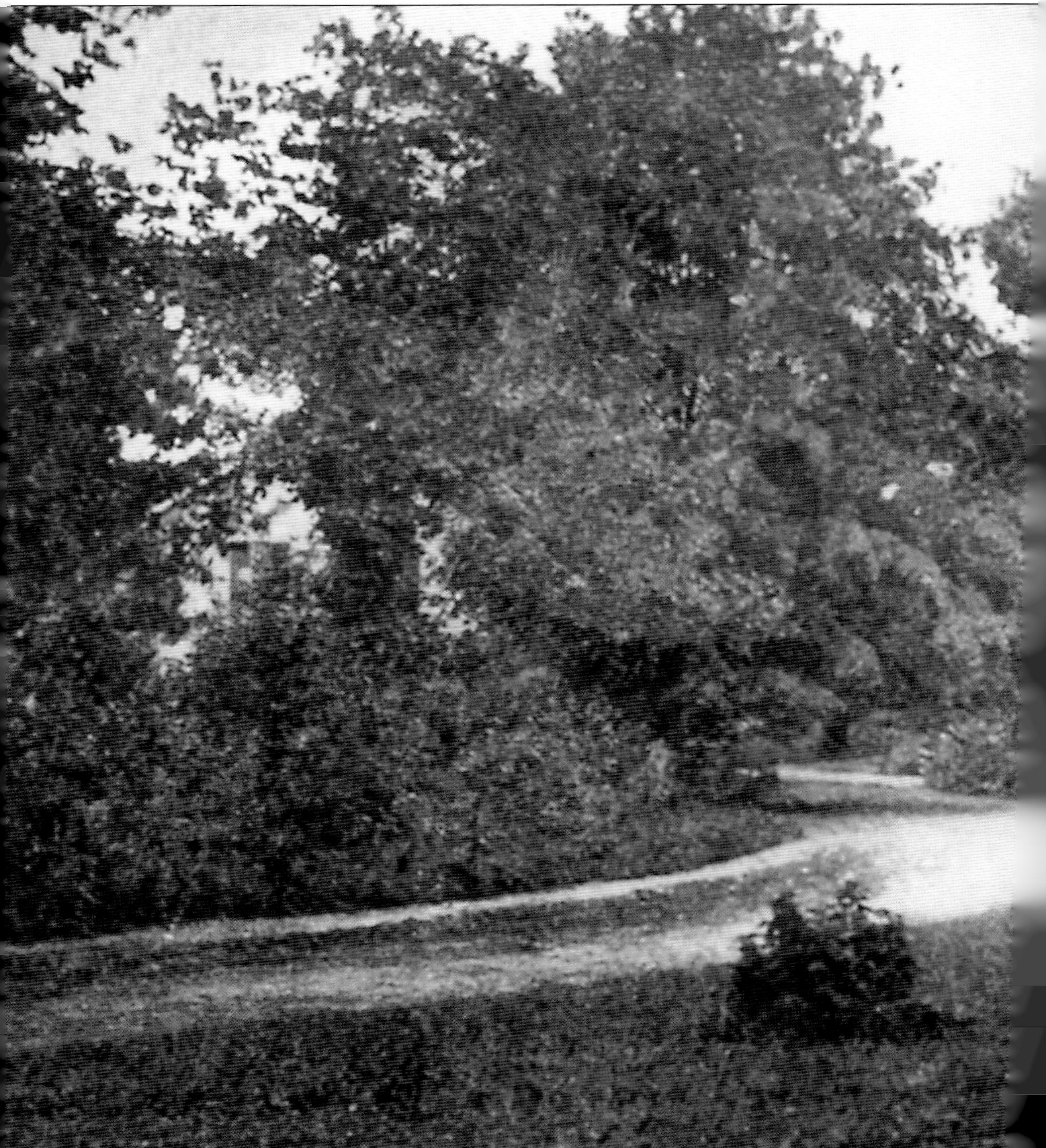

Wilton's original green was photographed from in front of what was once Keeler's Store, later King Real Estate. Going northeast, the road led across an iron bridge that crossed over the

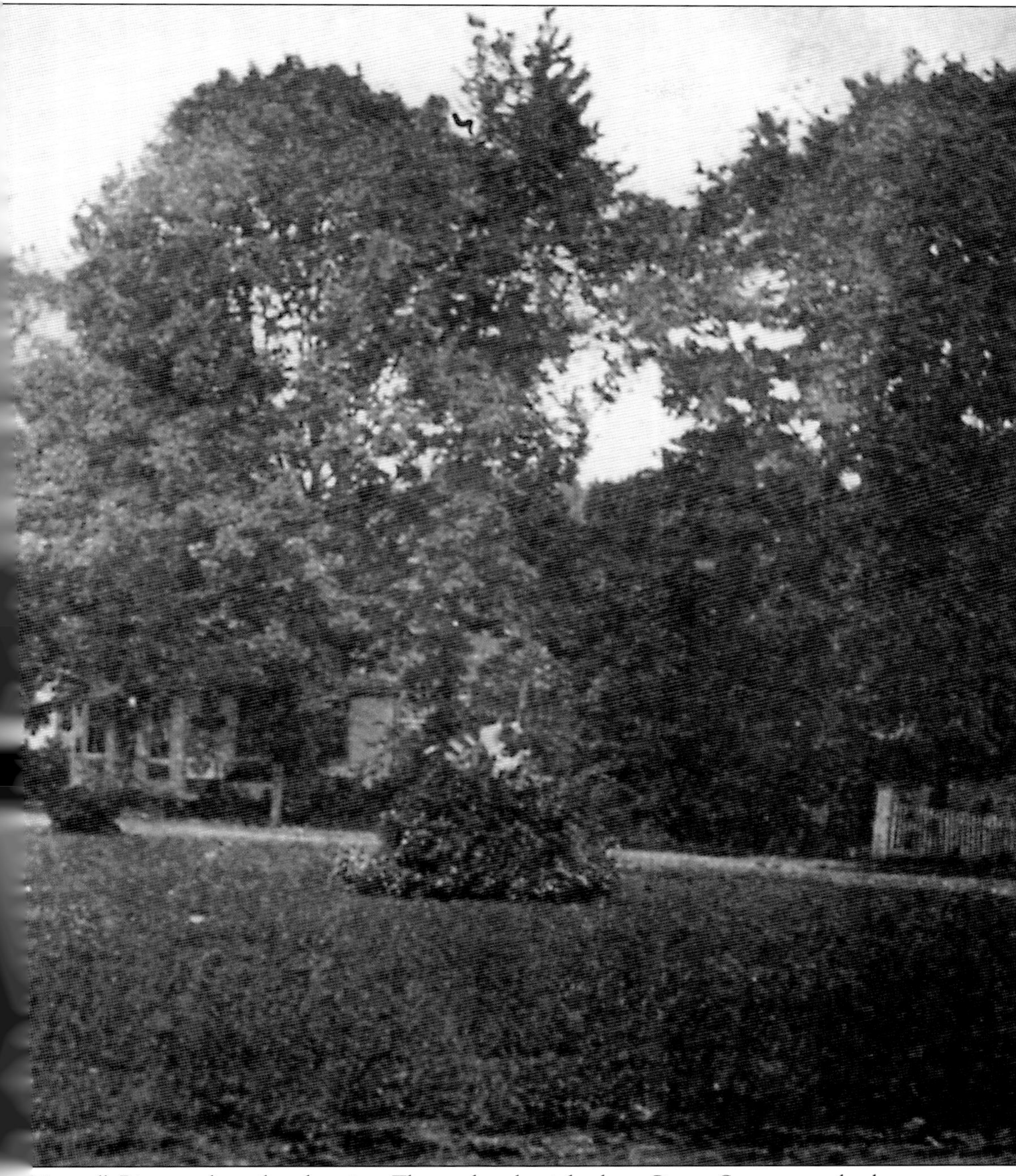

Norwalk River to the railroad station. The road to the right, later Center Street, went back over the river by another bridge and through to Danbury Road.

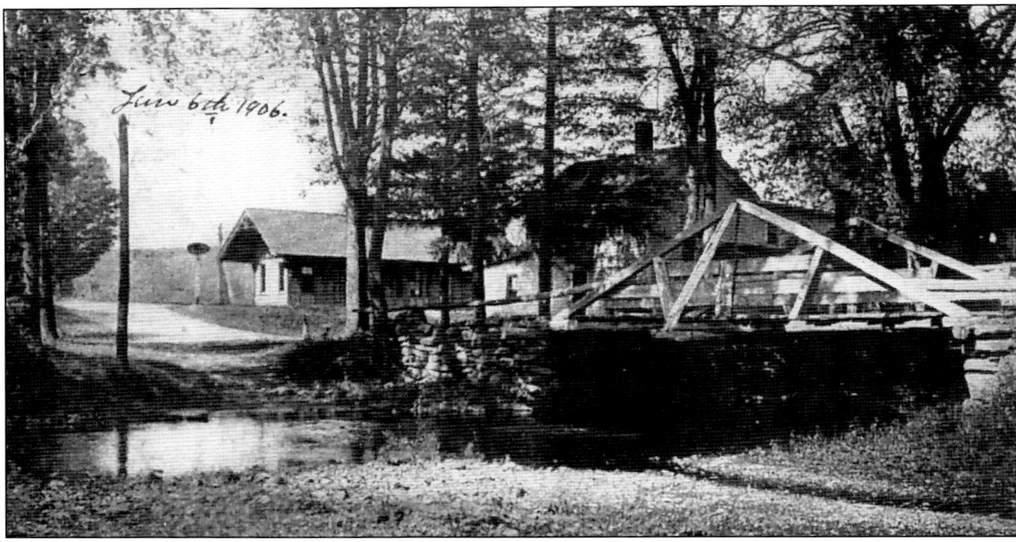

This postcard of Cannon's Station, postmarked January 1906, shows the old bridge that led to the community known variously as Cannon's, Cannon's Station, and then Cannondale. In this view are the railroad station, the home of Ralph Gregory and family, and the store and post office run for many years by members of that family.

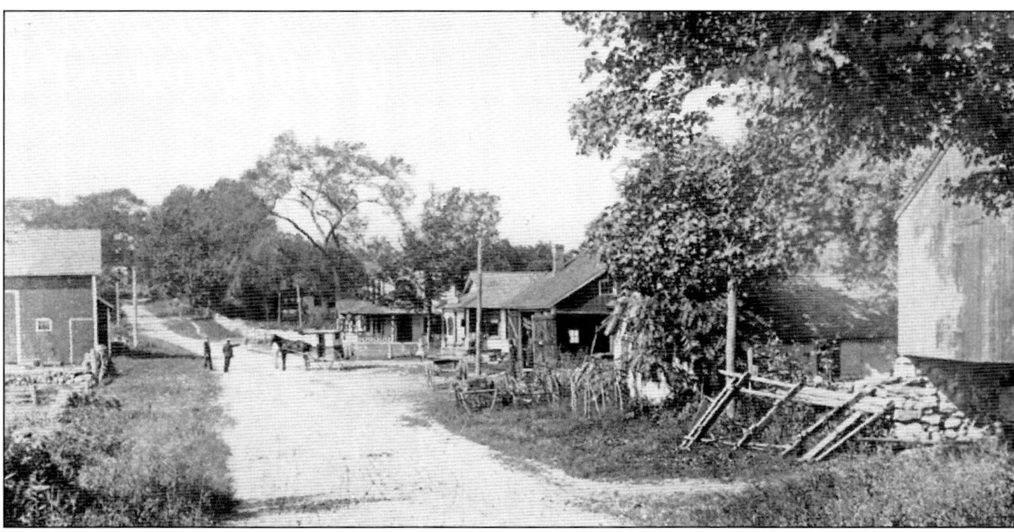

Hurlbutt Street, which contained another community cluster, had a store, a blacksmith shop, and a school. George B. Abbott had his blacksmith shop in the barn on the left. On the other side of the street was the general store run by Bedients and Barretts. It has been preserved at Lambert corners. Other residents of Hurlbutt Street cut ice, butchered meat, and made shoes. This view looks north from the corner of Sharp Hill Road and was published in 1906.

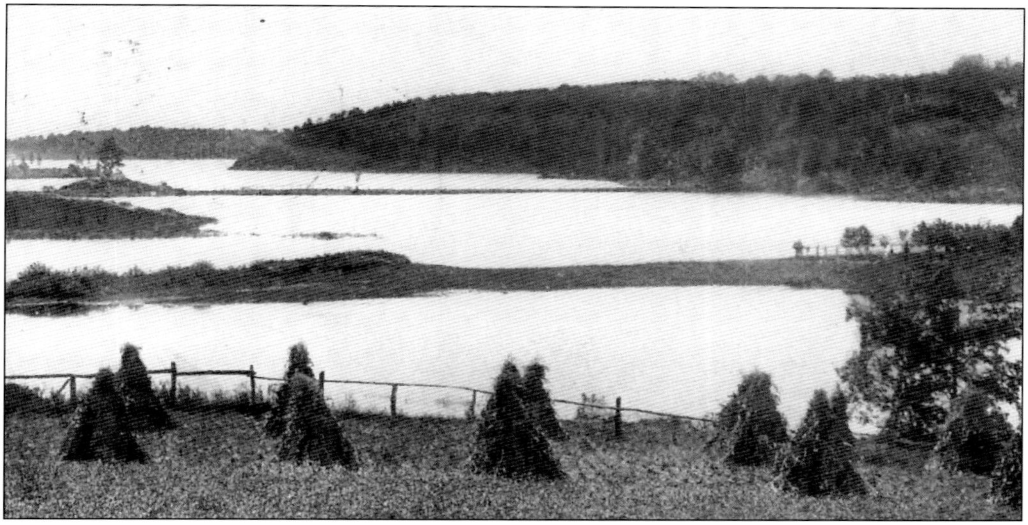

The 22-acre property used to create the South Norwalk Reservoir was bought in 1875 from Abijah M. and Elizabeth Law Jones. Before World War II, residents found the area a good place for fishing, botanizing, and hiking. It was abundant in plant and animal life.

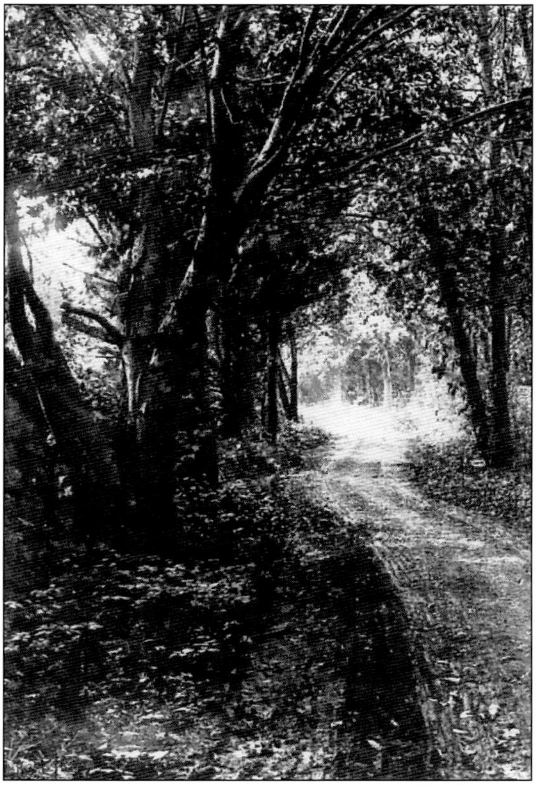

The road shown here is probably part of Grumman Hill Road. It connected the top of the hill to Kensett Avenue; a second version of the postcard, in color, calls it "The Road to the Kensett Sanitarium."

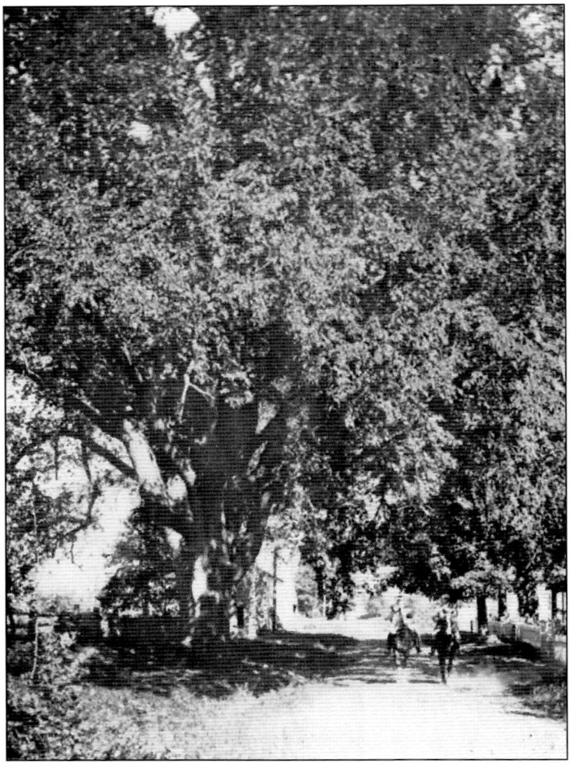

The Big Elm was on the west side of Belden Hill Road, just below the junction with New Canaan Road. It stood opposite the home of the Frank Benedict family, at 332 Belden Hill Road. One of the biggest trees in the state at the time, according to Daniel Sturges, it probably was demolished in 1936. That year's *Town Report* says that money was budgeted for the repair of Belden Hill and New Canaan Roads. The roadwork probably accounted for the tree's destruction.

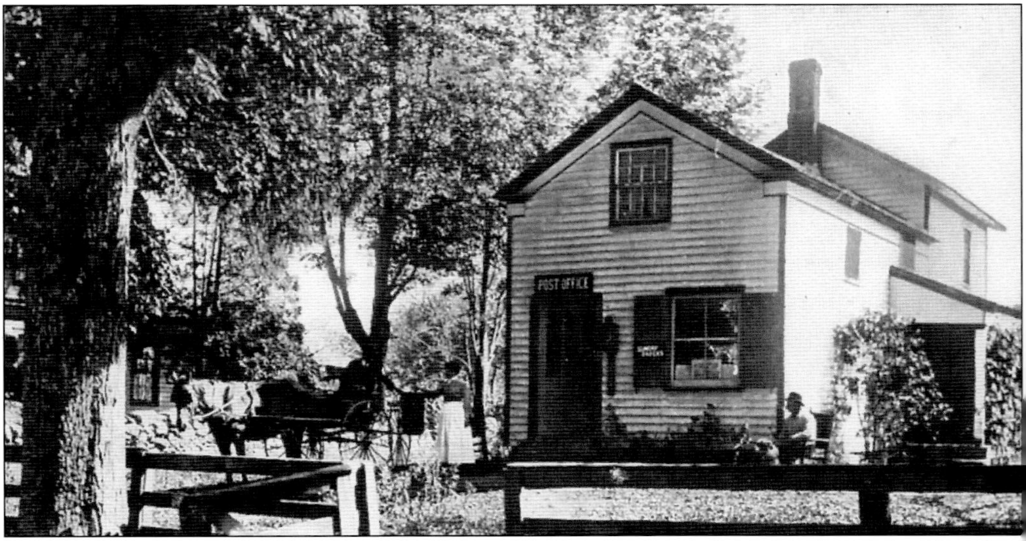

This post office was located just north of Kensett Avenue on Danbury Road. The building had also been a store and a home. The postmistress at that time was a Mrs. Davies. Other early post offices were at Wilton Center and at Bald and Nod Hills.

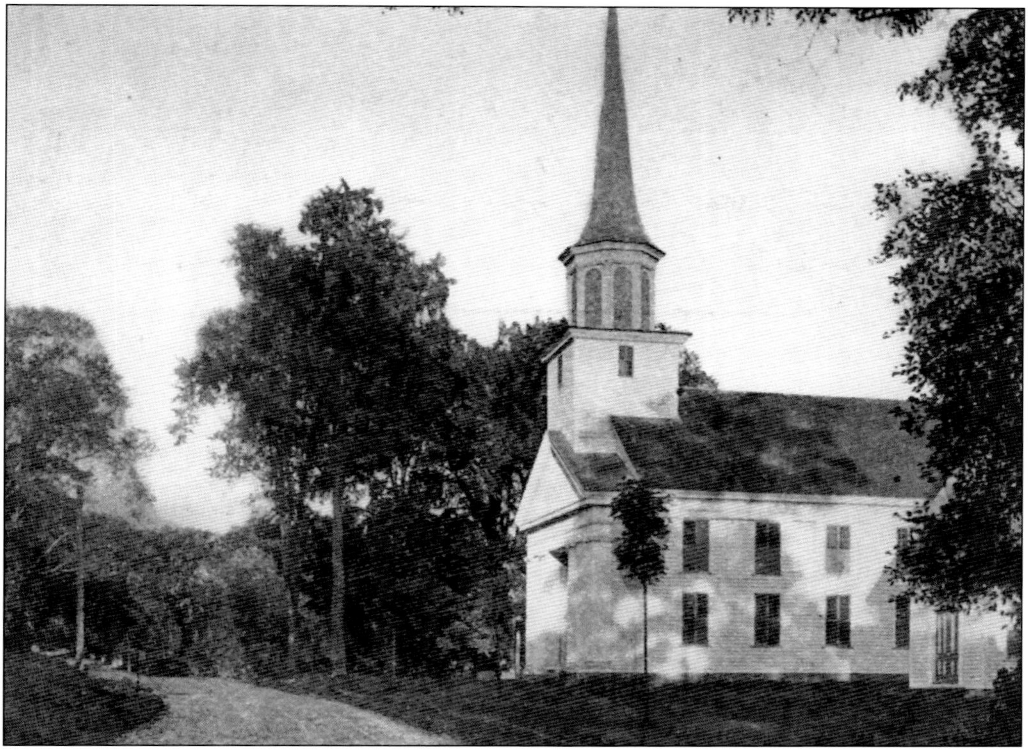

This was the third church building in Wilton for the Congregationalists. It was built in 1790. On the right is the parish hall that was built in 1871 and moved in 1952 to Lovers' Lane to become the Wilton Playshop. The current, larger parish hall was added later. This church has been the focus of images generated by several postcard companies.

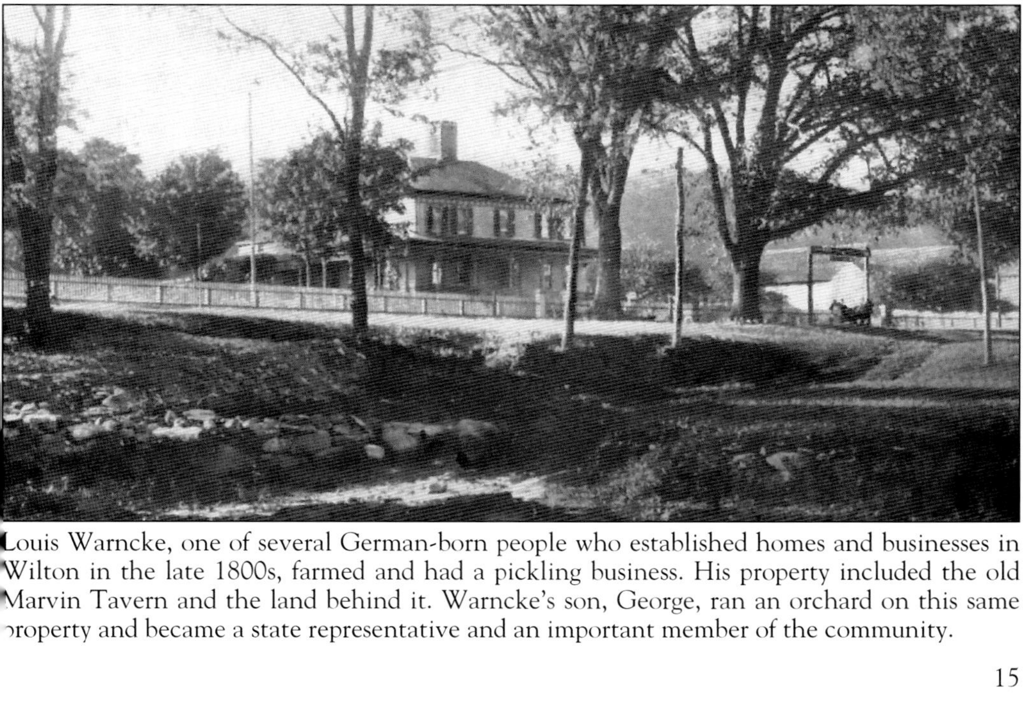

Louis Warncke, one of several German-born people who established homes and businesses in Wilton in the late 1800s, farmed and had a pickling business. His property included the old Marvin Tavern and the land behind it. Warncke's son, George, ran an orchard on this same property and became a state representative and an important member of the community.

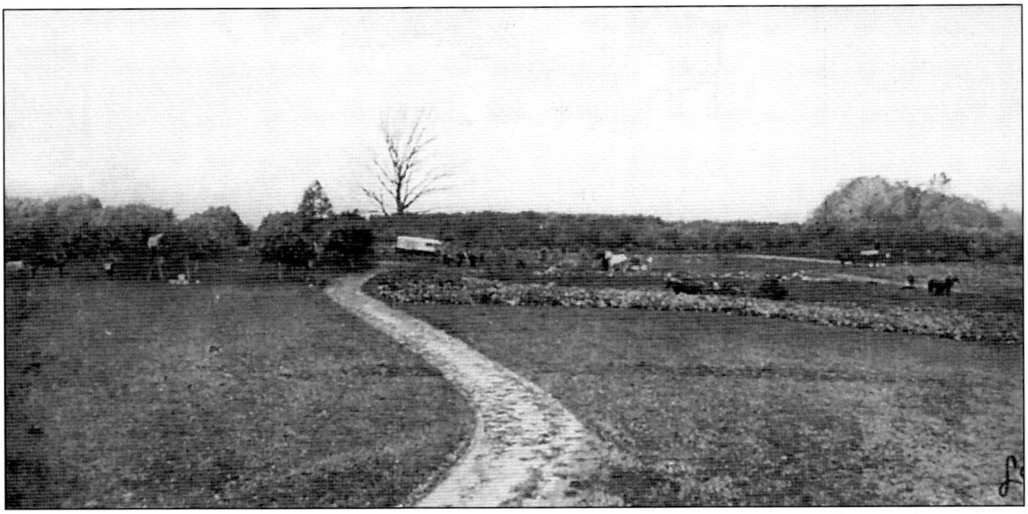

Orchards, gardens, houses, and farm buildings completed the Warncke's farm, where local residents went to buy produce and cider.

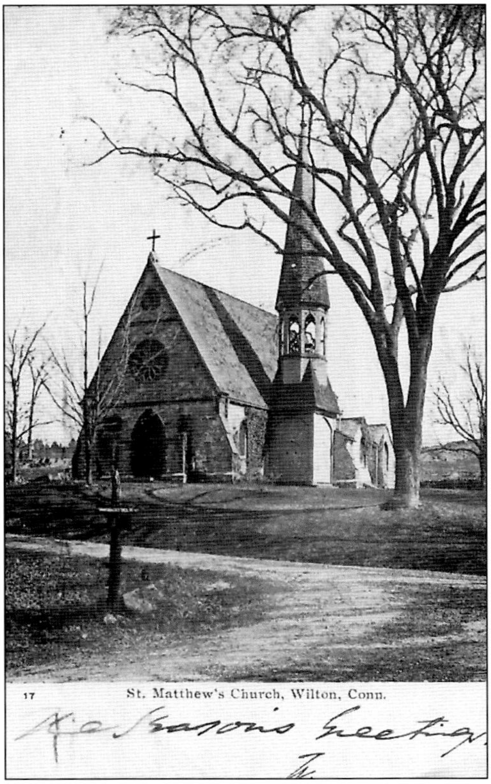

In the foreground, the hand-hewn sign points to Ridgefield. This road once crossed the railroad tracks and a wooden bridge into Wilton Center.

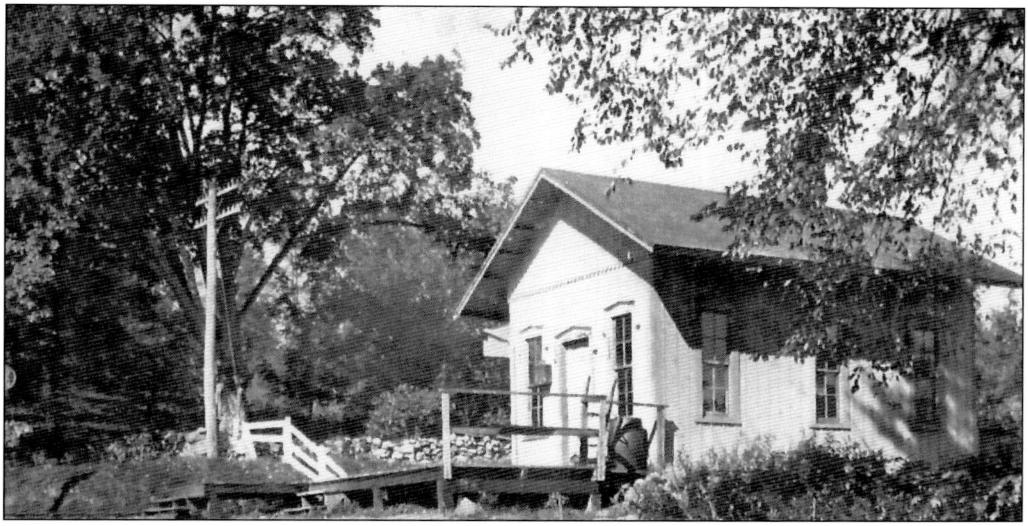

This small station was located on the north side of Kent Road as viewed from Danbury Road. It was also called Hopkins Station on an old timetable. Fred Hopkins was for many years station agent at the main Wilton station. Most recently, commuters stood in a small metal shed when waiting for a train.

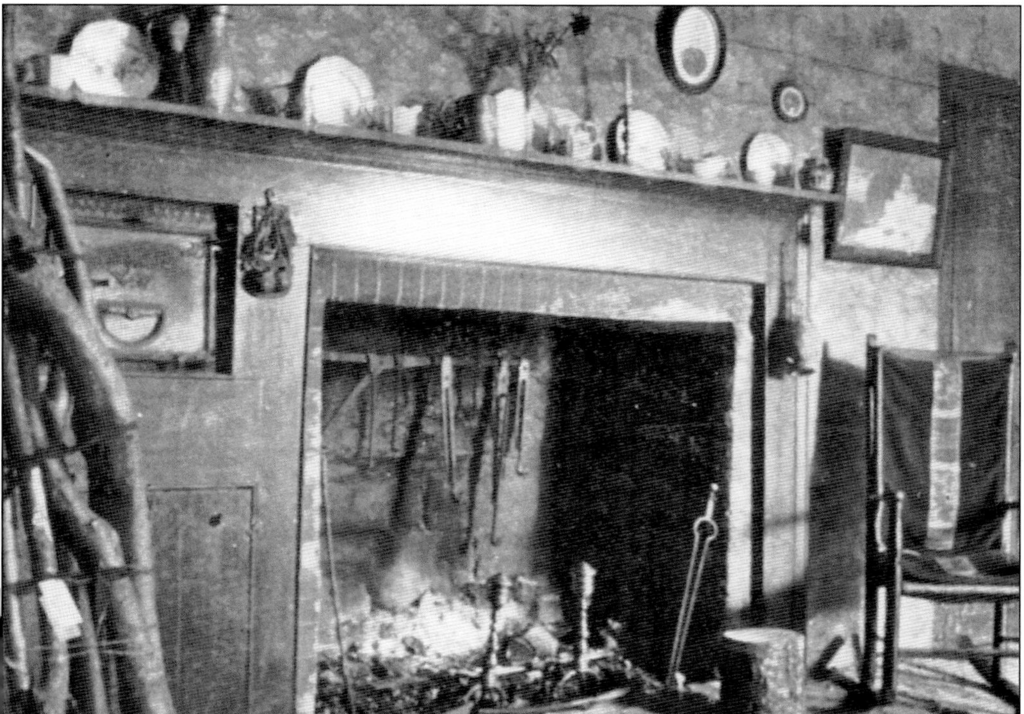

This is the fireplace from the original kitchen of the Sloane-Raymond-Fitch House, now the Wilton Heritage Museum belonging to the Wilton Historical Society. The house, given by Ralph Piersall, is at 249 Danbury Road. It has been restored and is the society's headquarters. It was the Fitch family homestead for a hundred years.

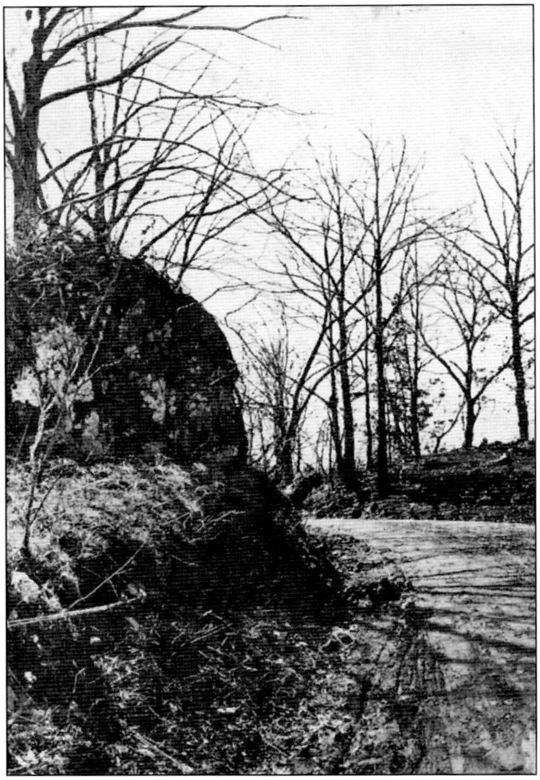

Poison Rock was so called because it was always covered with poison ivy, according to David Van Hoosear, Wilton historian. It was on the west side of Danbury Road near the top of the hill when viewed from the junction with Route 33.

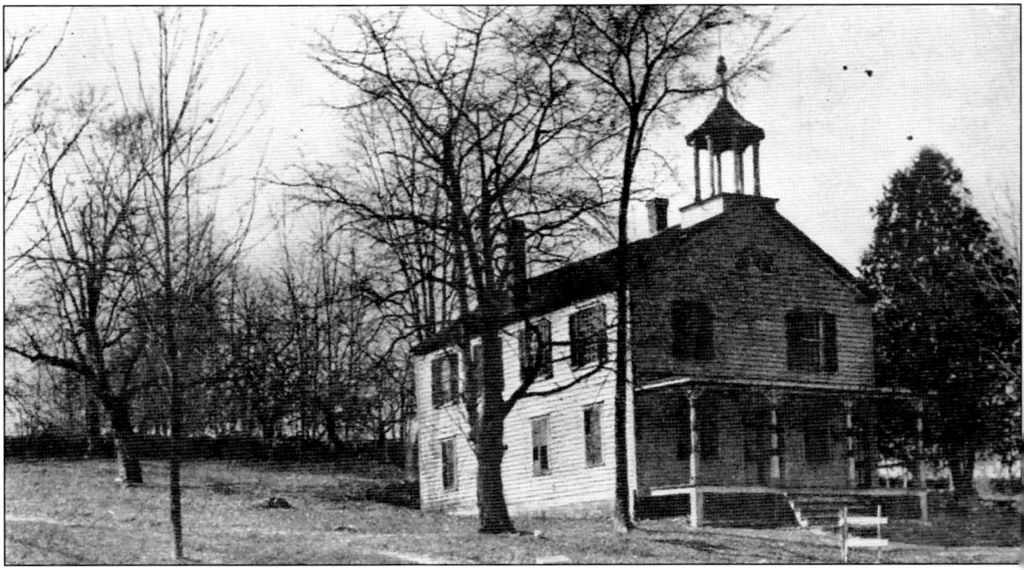

Wilton's first town hall has served several purposes since it was built in 1828–29. The building has been the site of town meetings and the private Wilton Academy of Hawley Olmstead, and it once served as a temporary classroom for town pupils.

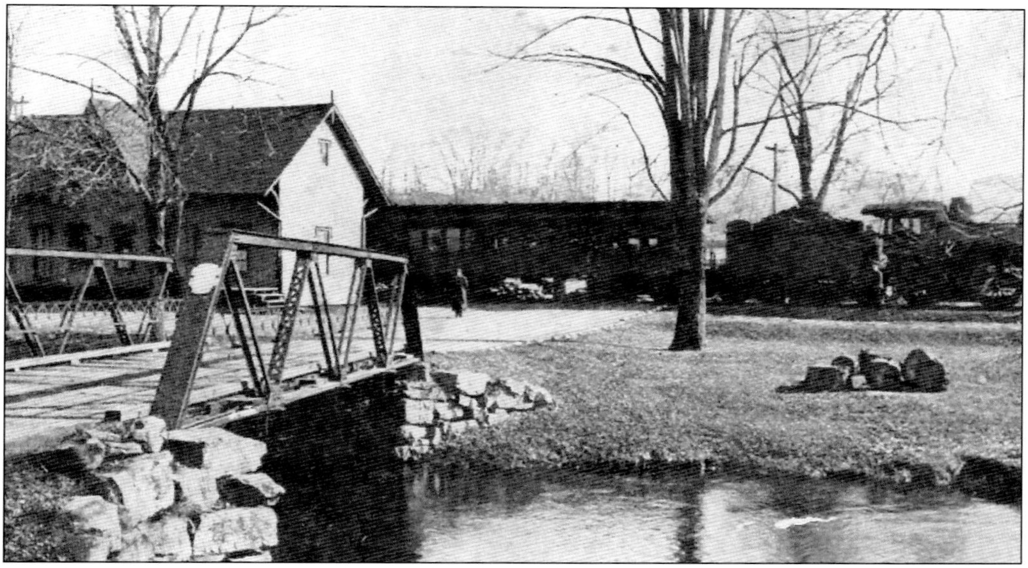

This is Wilton's original train station. The bridge crossed the Norwalk River coming from the green at Wilton Center. The approach to Danbury Road is beyond the train waiting for its passengers.

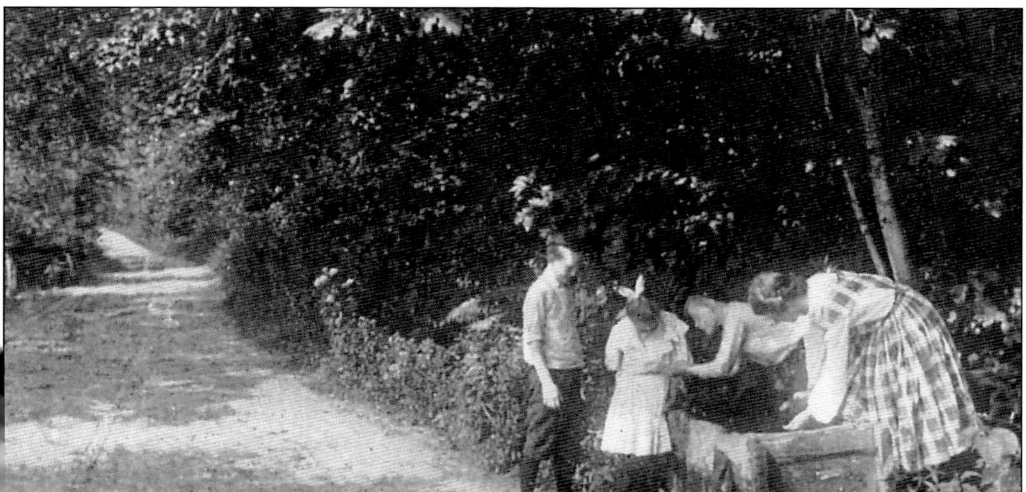

'n the days of horse-powered transportation, several watering troughs were found throughout .own, particularly at the bottom of hills such as Sharp Hill and Belden Hill. Children apparently ·njoyed these as much as the horses.

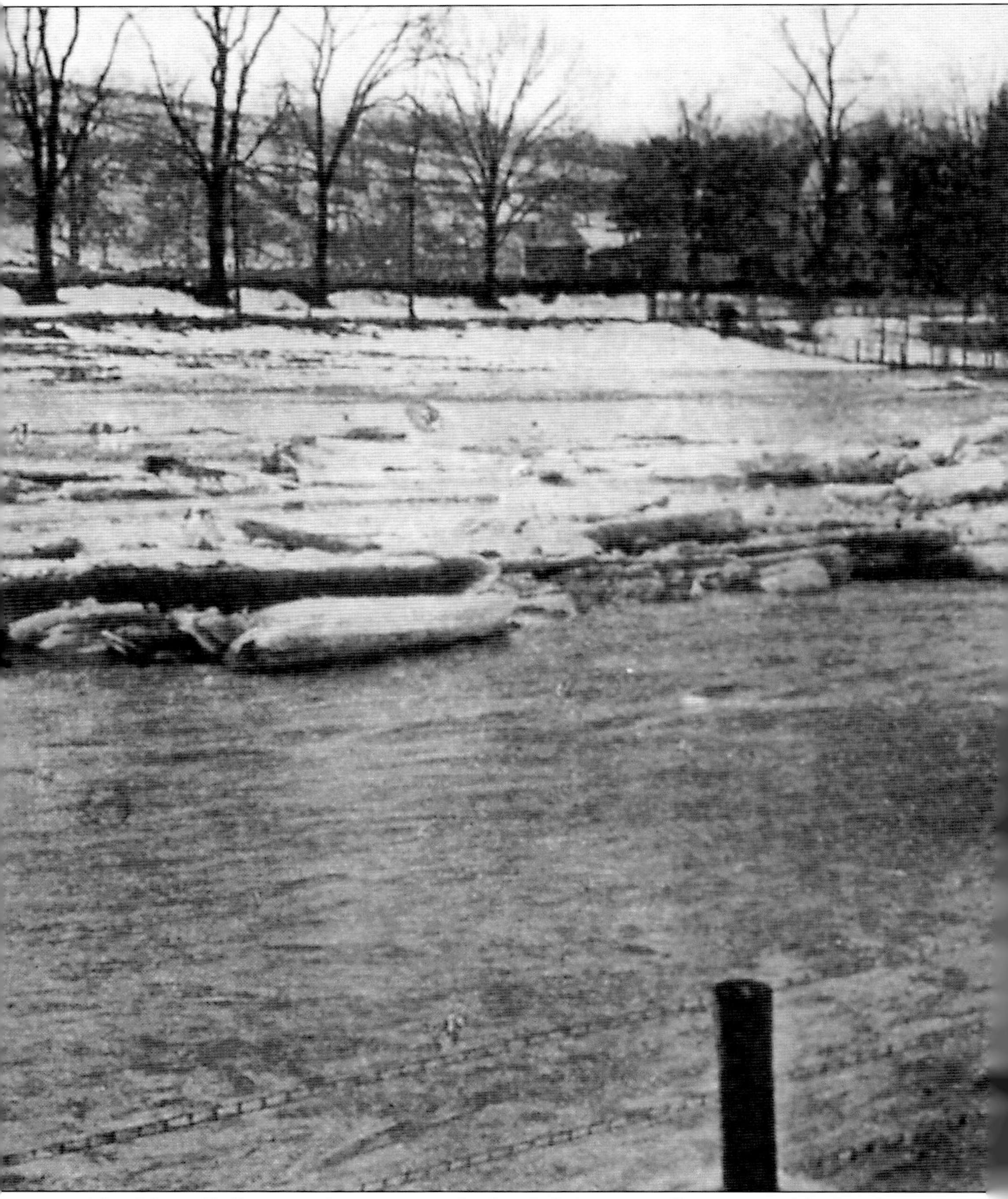

The Norwalk River is shown not only flooded, but with floating ice blocks. On Cottage Row are the houses of Anna Carpenter, George Heddin, Ethel Hart, and George Taylor.

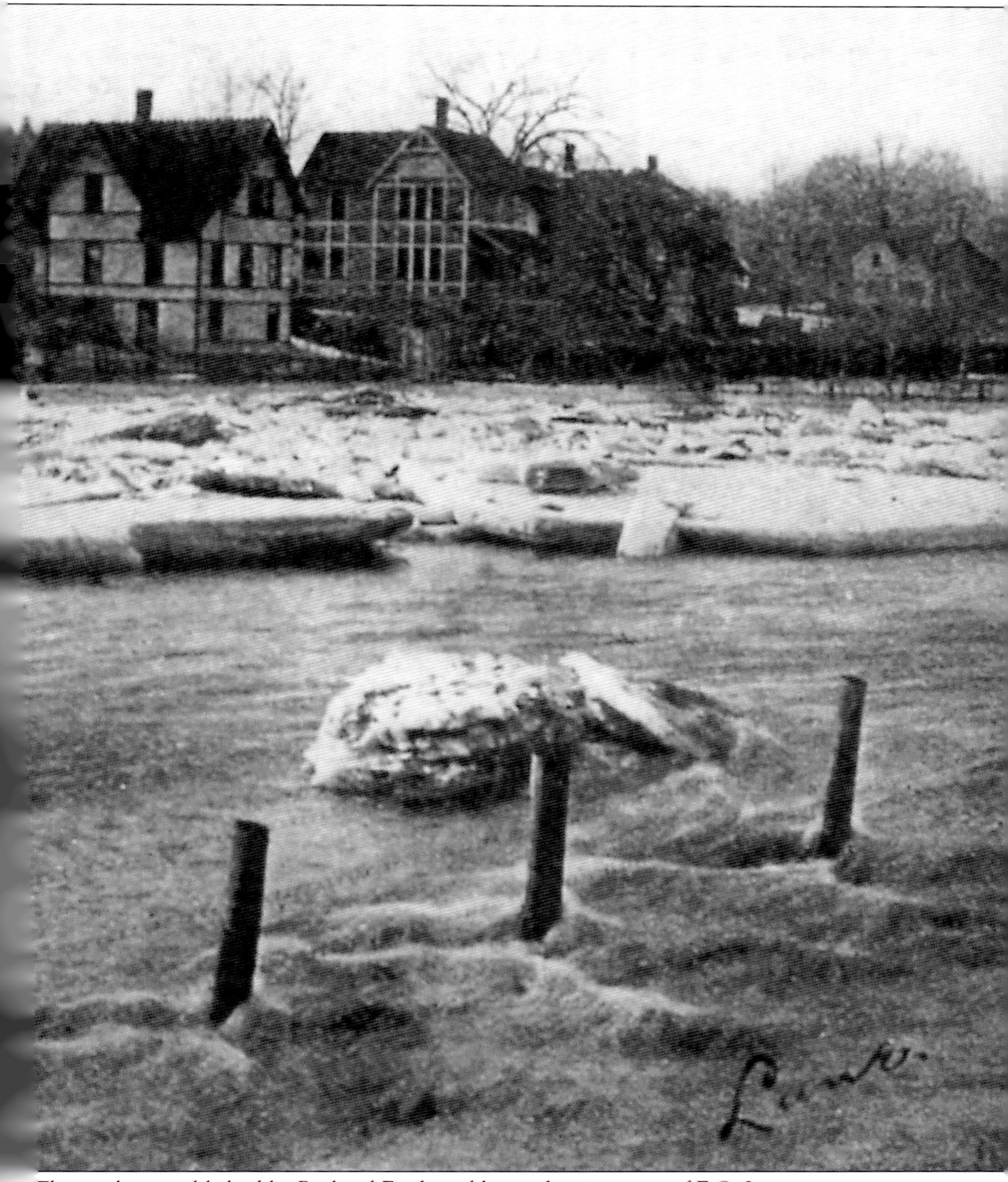

The card was published by Richard Fitch and bears the signature of F.G. Lane.

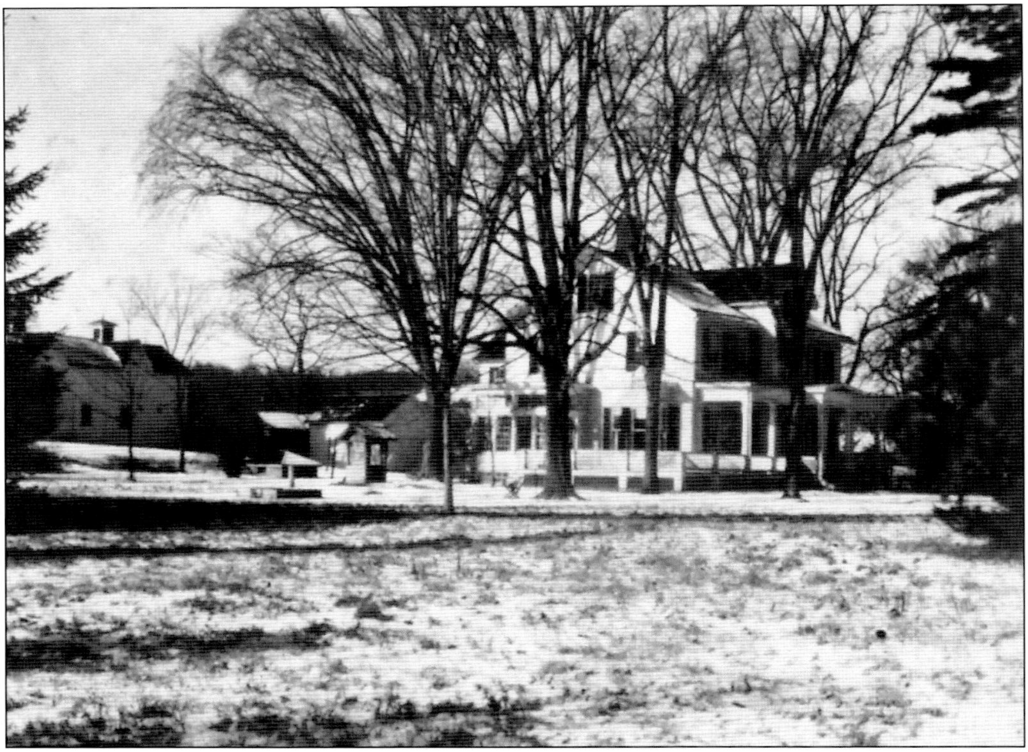

The house of the Ethel Betts Weston family stood across from Deerfield Road. The site has been home to a furniture store, a bank, and a publishing company since the house was torn down.

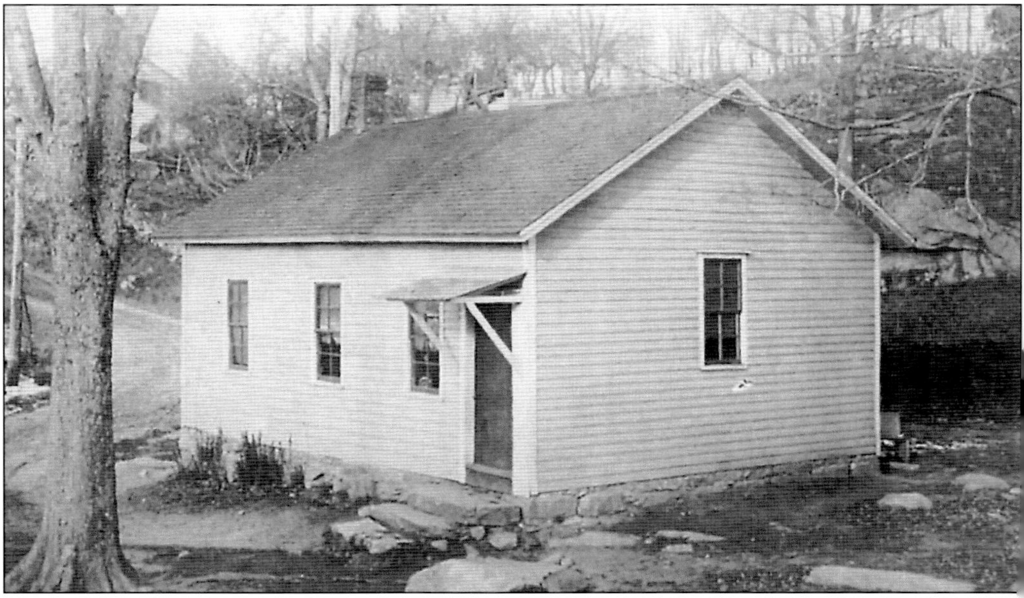

This small school, built on the triangle at the intersection of Drum Hill Road and Belden Hil[l] Road, was once referred to as the "flop-in, flop-out school" because of its small size with door[s] at each side. It was closed in 1915.

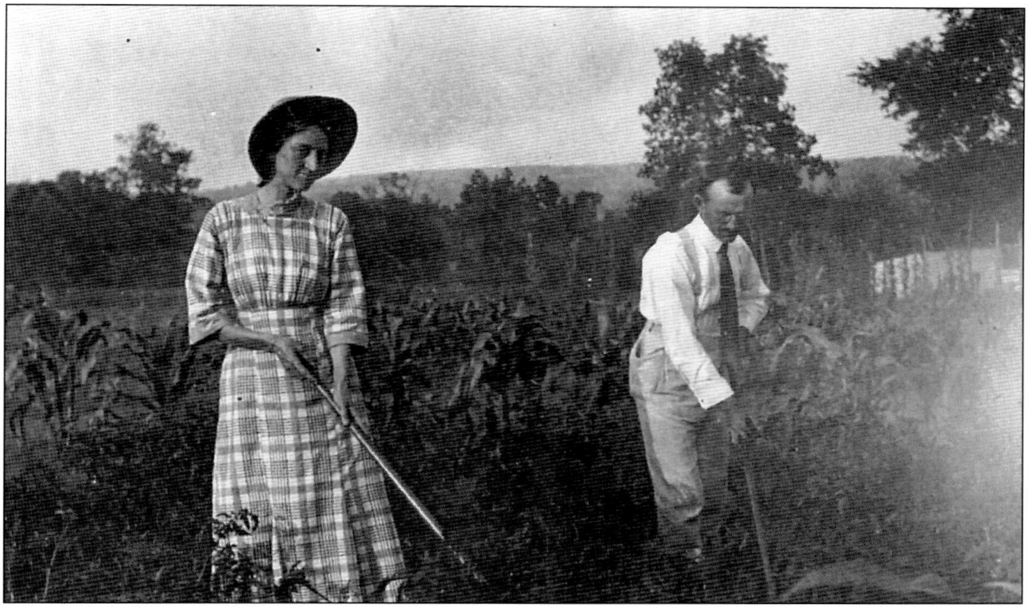

Although it depicts an inappropriate choice of clothing for gardening, this picture nevertheless gives a clear impression of Wilton's agricultural past.

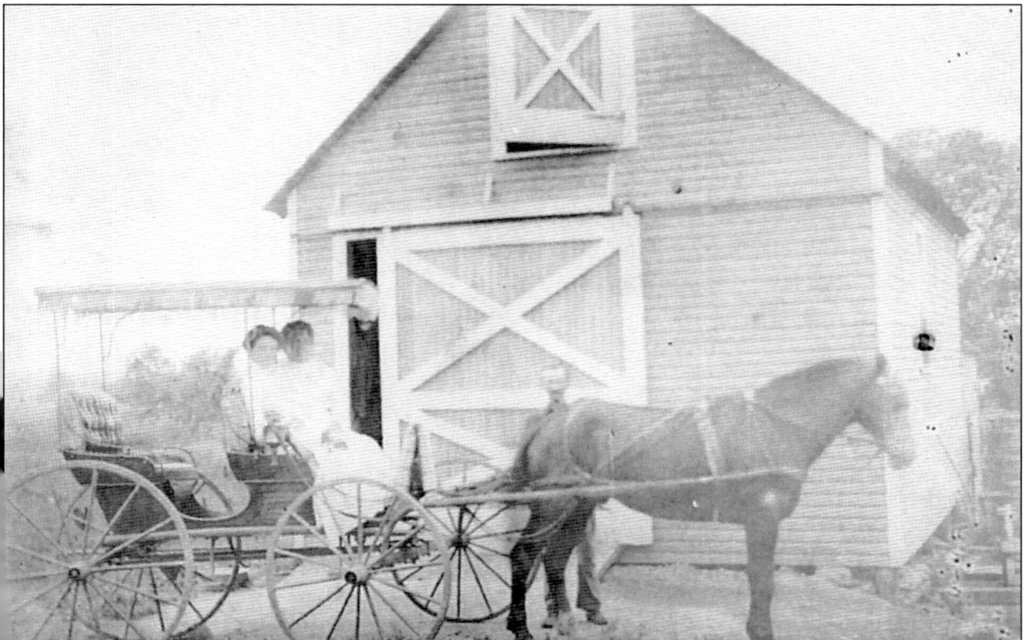

The horse, buggy, and small barn further illustrate Wilton's farming heritage.

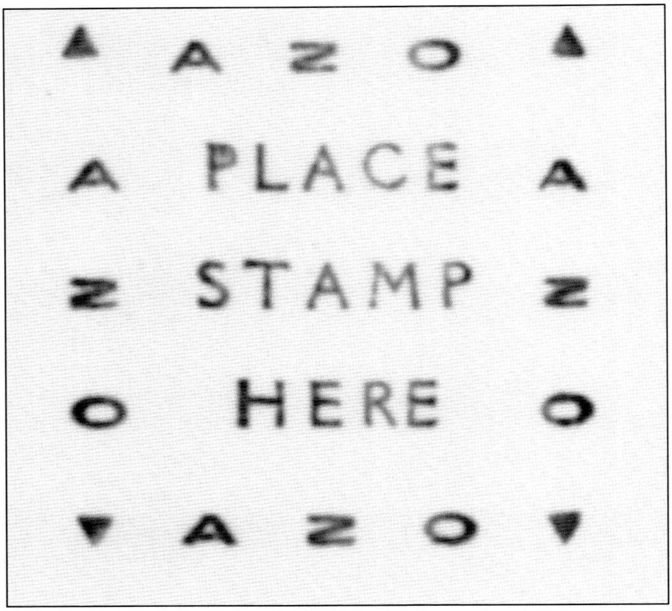

Many of the early postcards show this logo on the reverse side. It indicates the use of a photographic paper available to amateur cameramen for printing their own pictures as postcards.

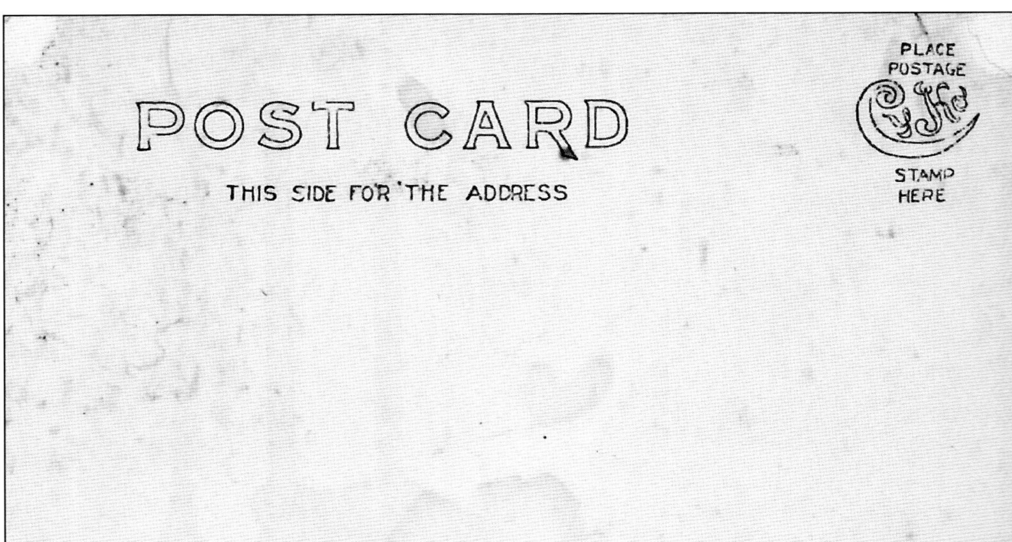

This seems to be an unidentified logo of an early postcard company, whose initials are worked into an ornate scroll.

Two

Mixed Methods

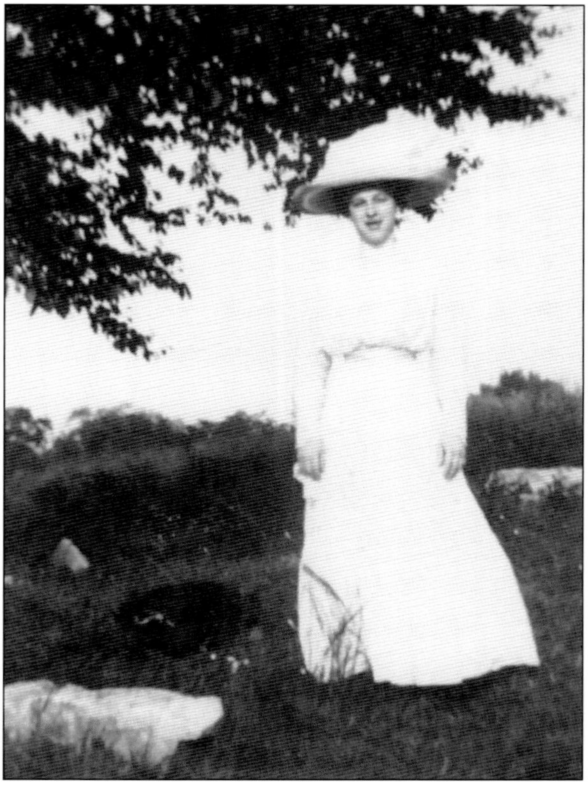

‹atherine Jane Abbott Bradley, nother and grandmother of the uthors, was recorded in this ome-style printed postcard.

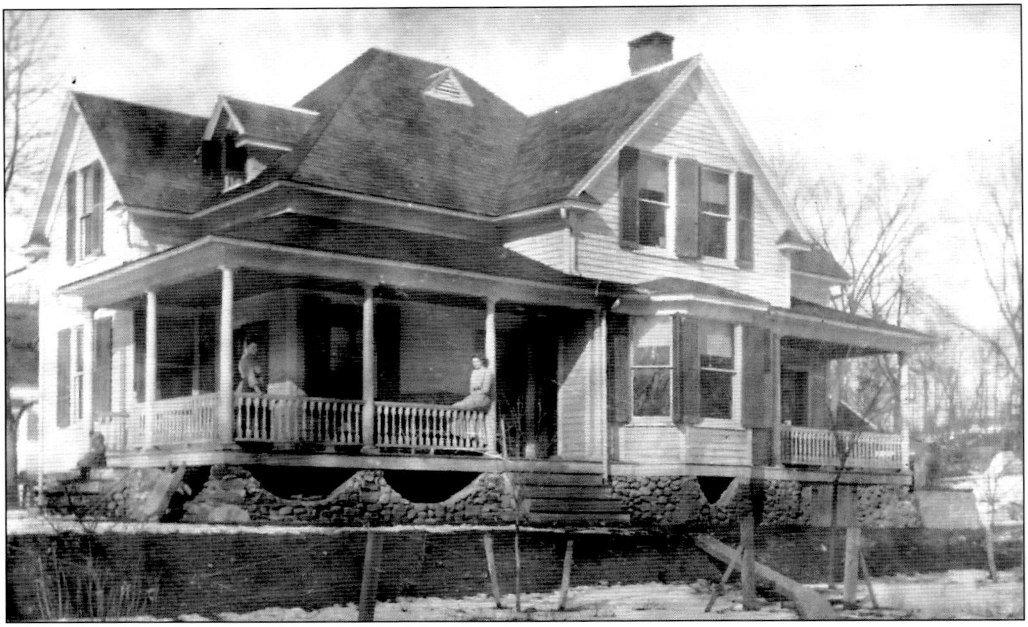

The new home of Almon C. Bradley, built around 1906, was within walking distance of the railroad station where he was station master. The house was sold in 1911 to Frederick Hopkins, the next agent, who lived there until the house was torn down to build an electric generator.

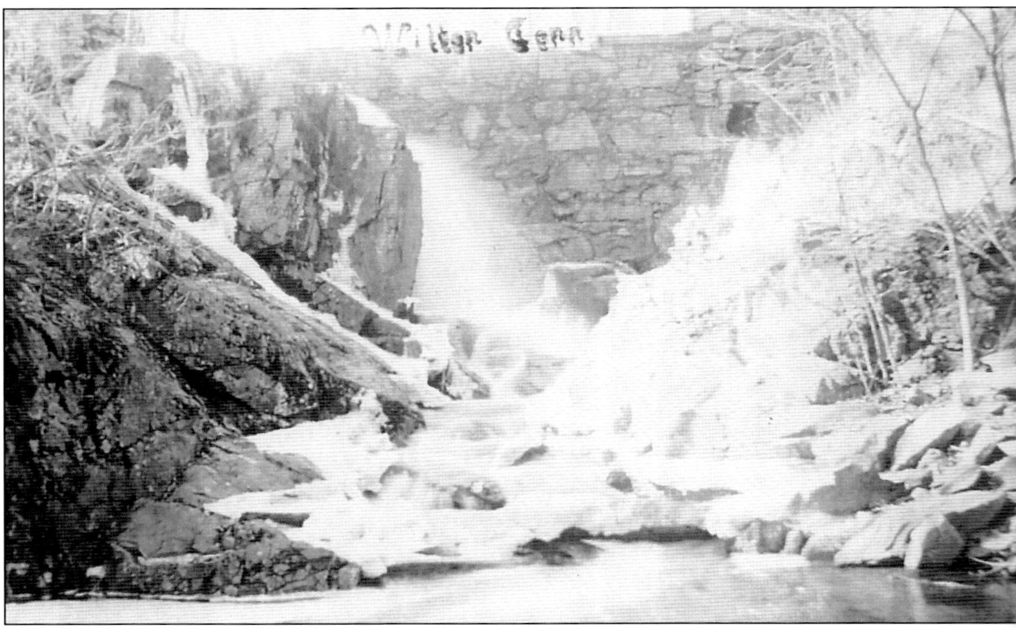

The usefulness of the old mill dams may have subsided, but their attraction for local postcard makers continued.

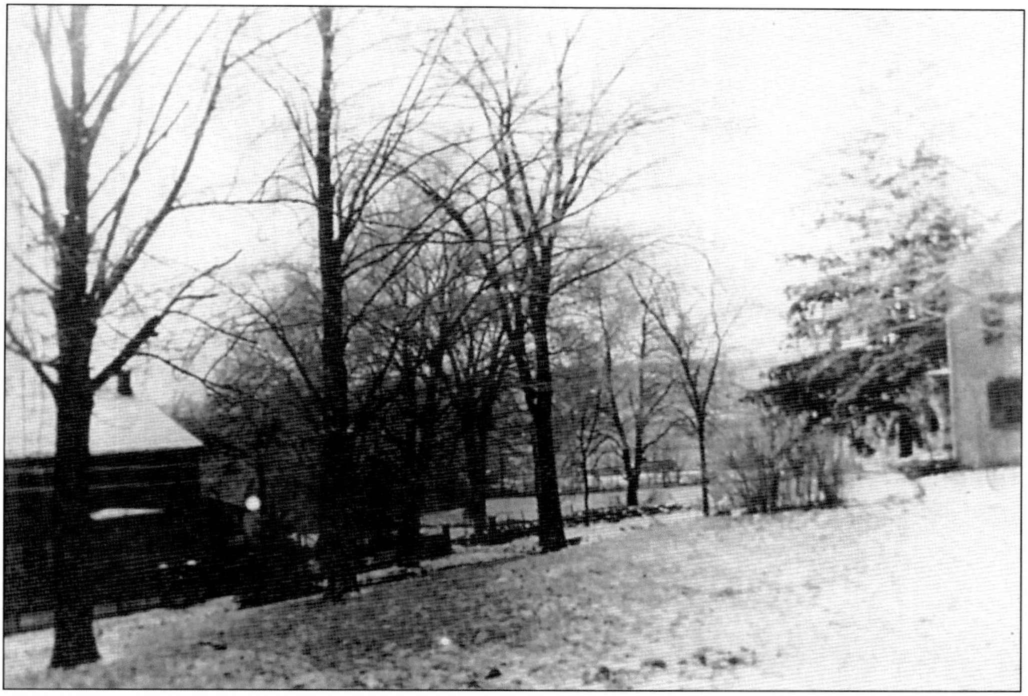

This appears to be a former view in Wilton Center.

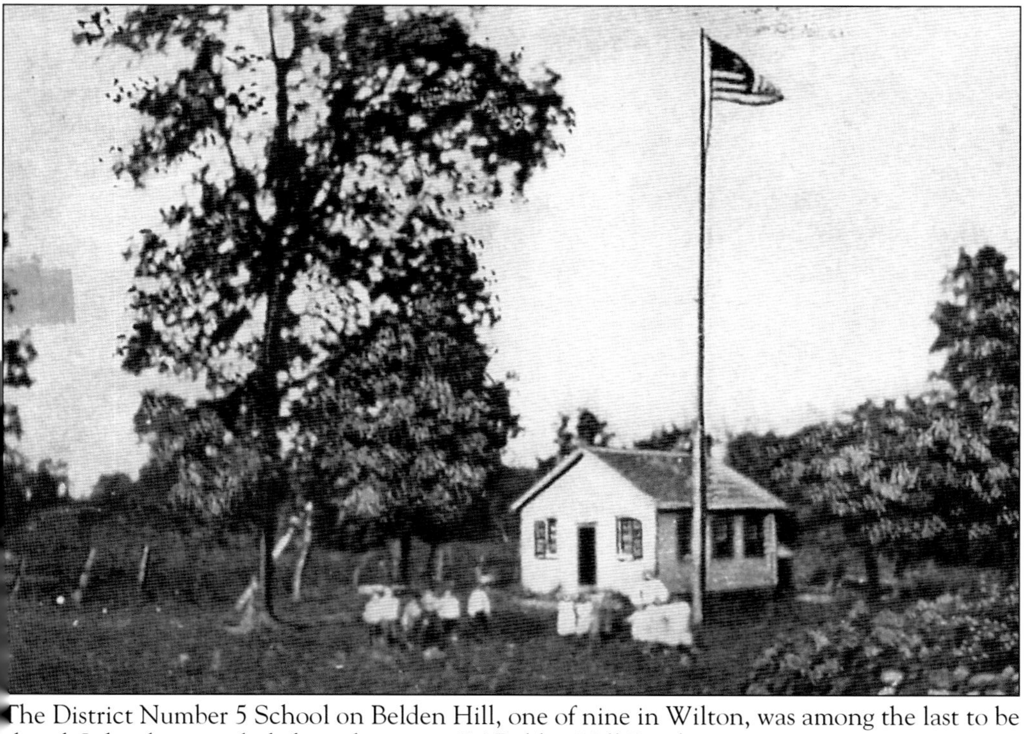

The District Number 5 School on Belden Hill, one of nine in Wilton, was among the last to be closed. It has been included in a house at 424 Belden Hill Road.

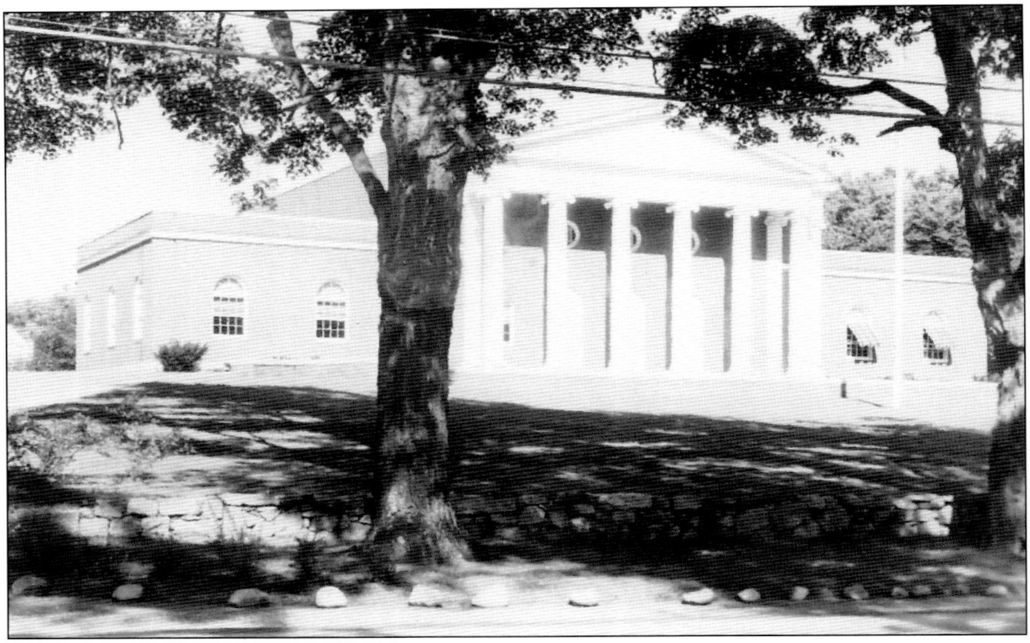

Wilton's "new" town hall was built on the site of the home of Reverend and Mrs. Charles A. Marks. Marks was minister of St. Matthew's Episcopal Church from 1906 to 1919. Shown here is one of several similar views. The former Shoff property, which has become a part of the town administrative area, is shown at the rear.

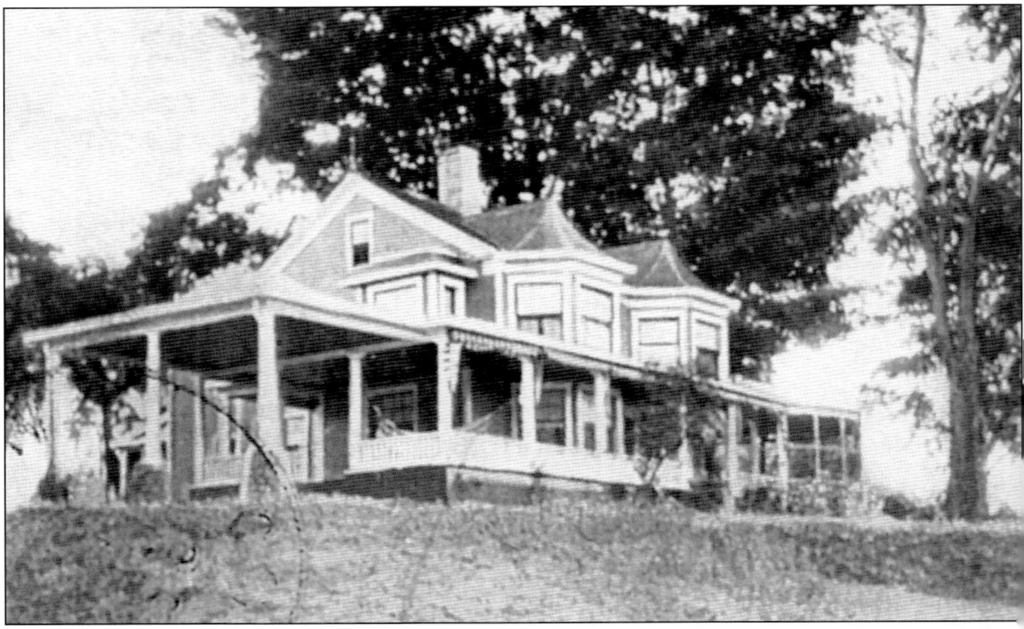

Property deeds show that Colonel W.R. Fearne and his wife, Doretta, first leased and then bought this house, some farm buildings, a large amount of property, and the right to use a boat on the nearby pond in 1903.

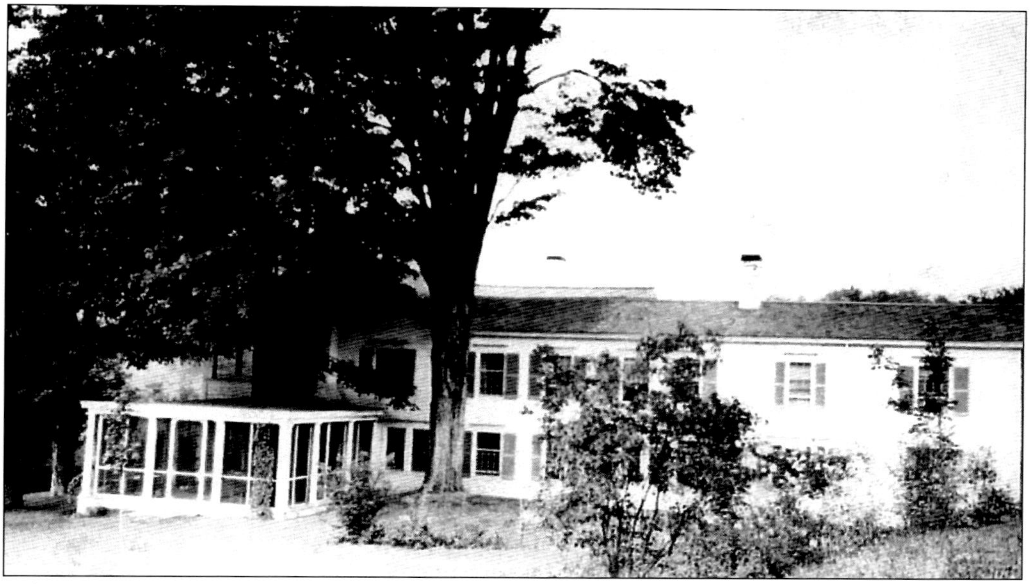

Ralph Rounds and family owned this large estate known as Dumplin Hill. The estate's name is said to derive from the actions of disgruntled workers who used their lunch dumplings for slingshot projectiles.

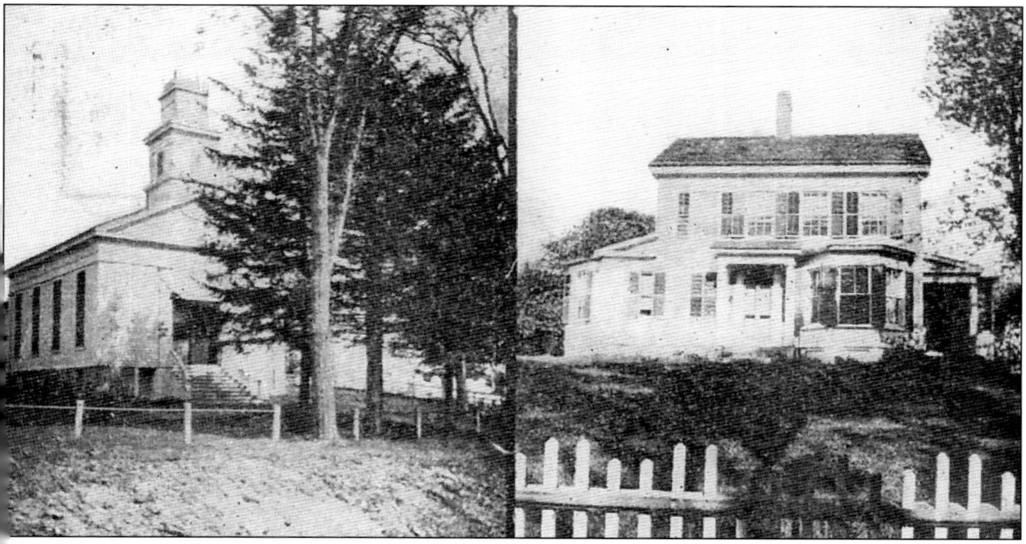

This unusual, double-view card shows Zion Hill Methodist Church (dedicated in 1844) and its longtime parsonage. The basic structures have changed little since this card was mailed in 1912.

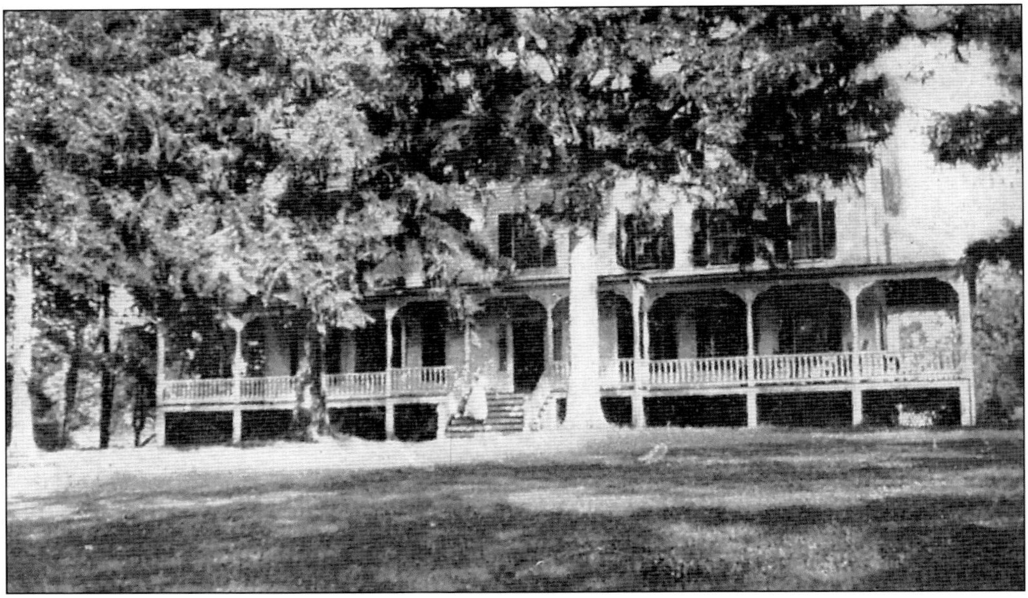

The Deaconess Rest Home was a retreat center for the Methodist church. It was located near the junction of Cannon Road and Pimpewaug Road and was formerly a private school run by Mr. and Mrs. Benjamin Brown.

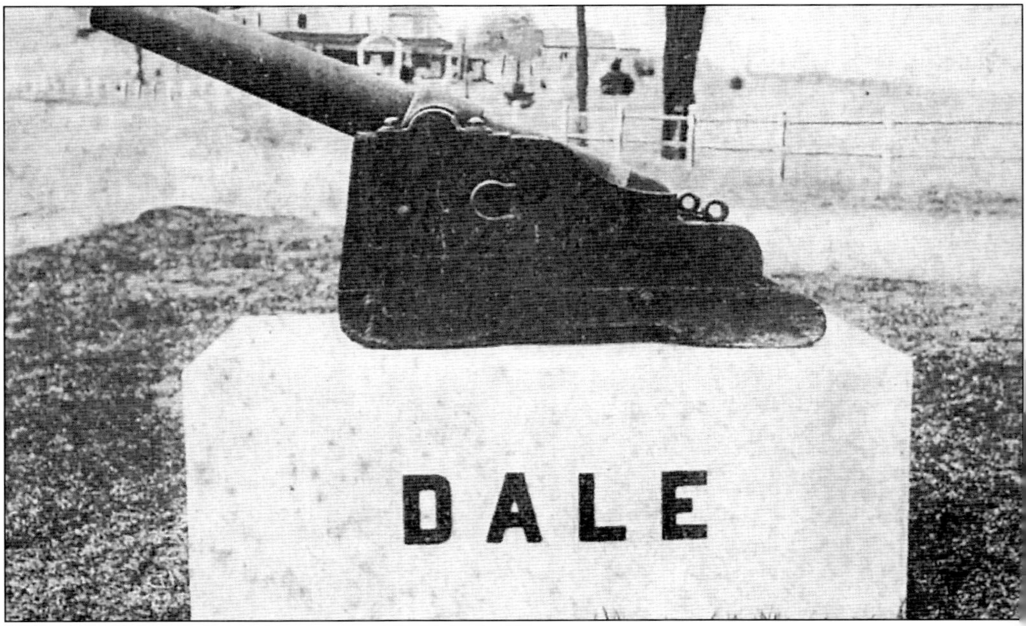

This cannon was given to the Cannon family in 1904. It came from the Battle of Galveston in the Civil War and stands now at the corner of Cannon Road and Danbury Road. The Cannons were merchants of Norwalk and Wilton and intermarried with the Miller family.

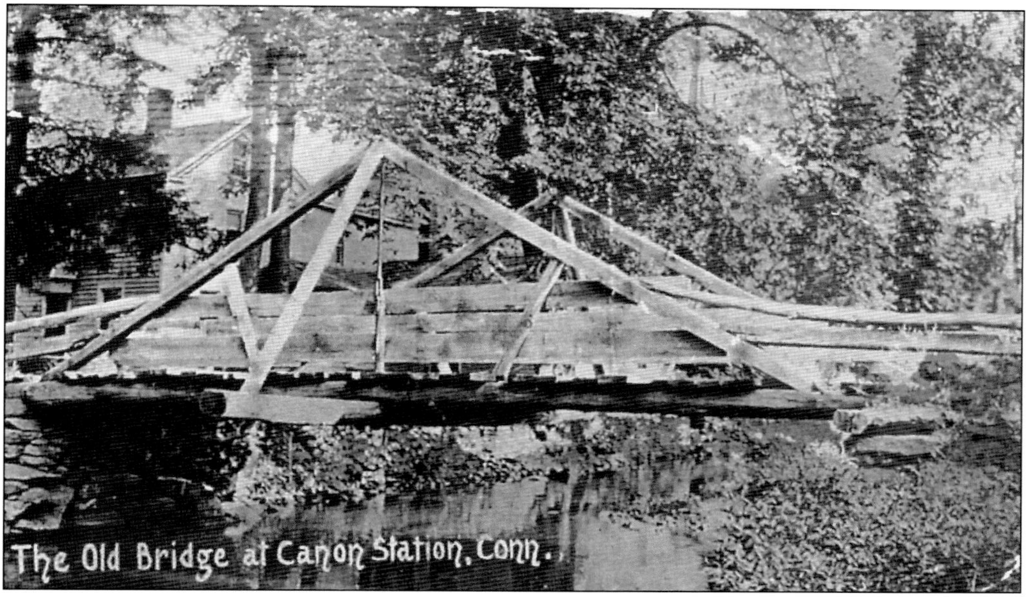

The bridge at Cannon Station appears very fragile in this card made by the A. Pearson Co. under the Defender logo.

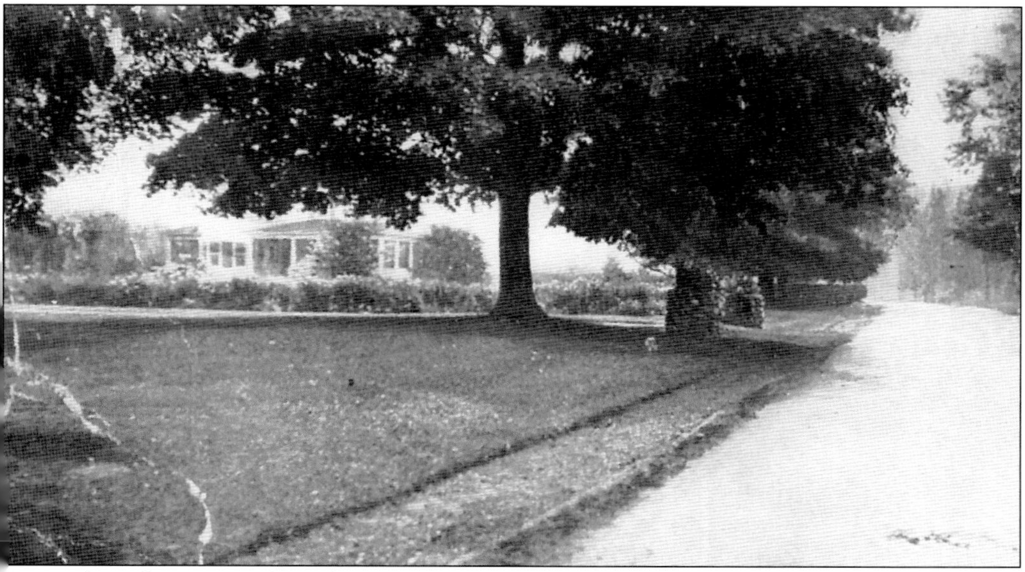

Pictured in this postcard is what appears to be the former Miller-Ambler-Cannon property. The view commemorates the important commercial contributions of the Cannon family of the Civil War era.

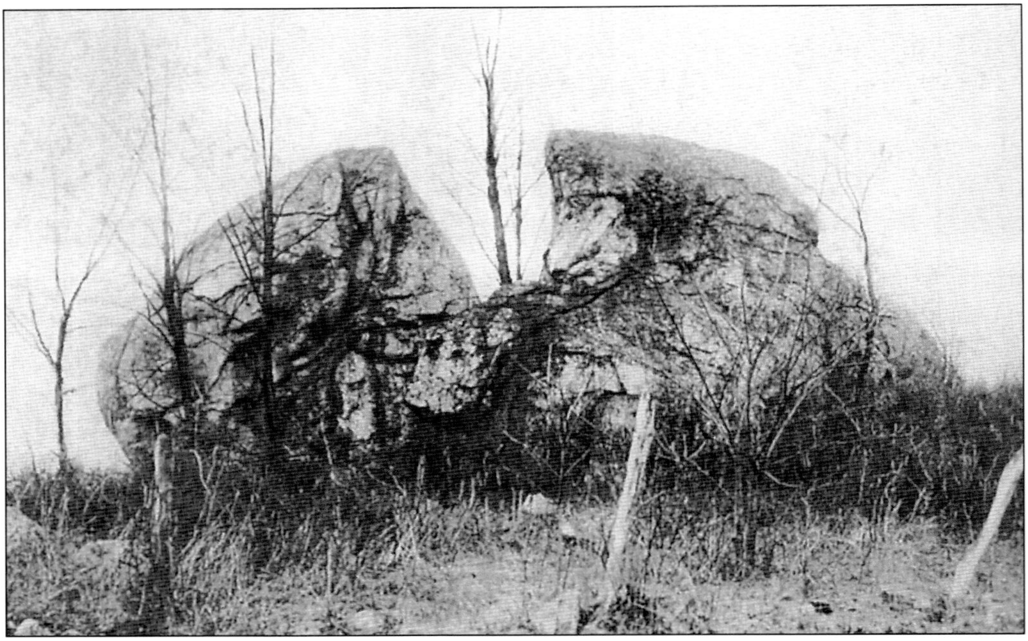

The Split Rock, a natural formation near the corner of Scribner Hill Road, was once on the property of a large farm known as Egypt. The farm was so named because its crops thrived when others failed.

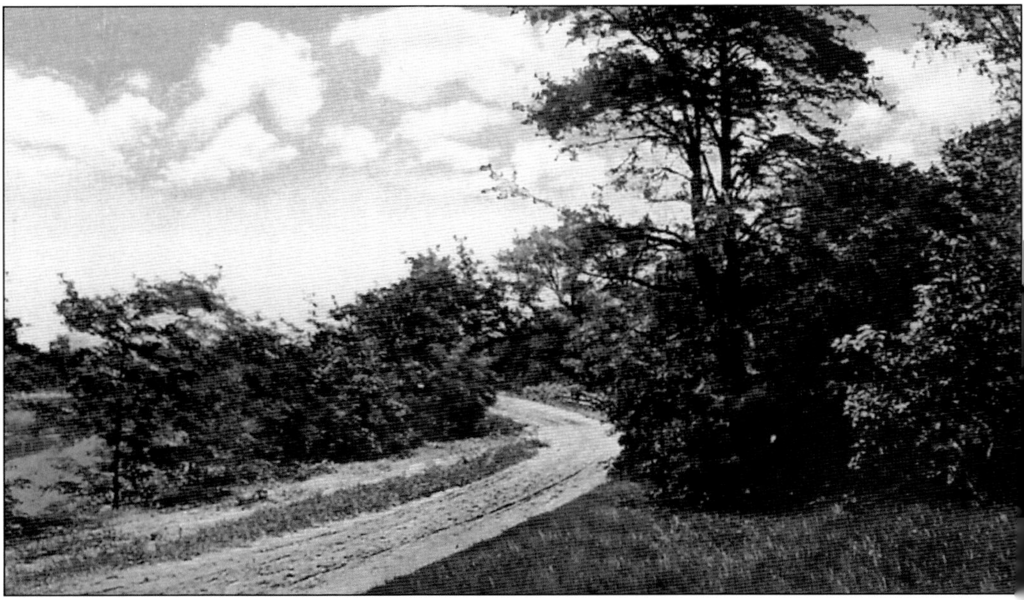

The greeting was warm but the location is no longer identifiable.

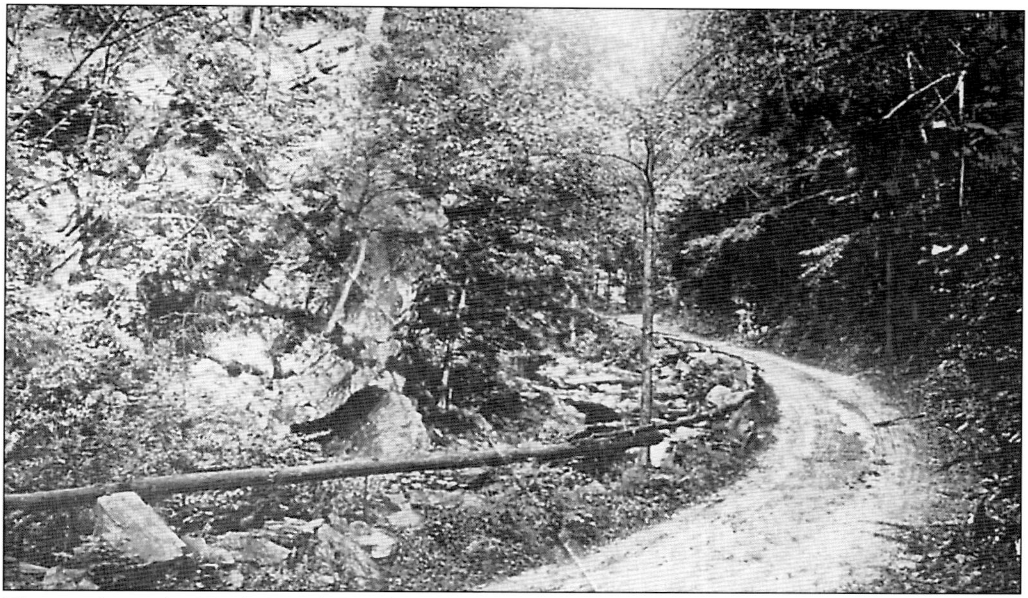

This road runs by Knob Crook Brook in the northern part of Georgetown.

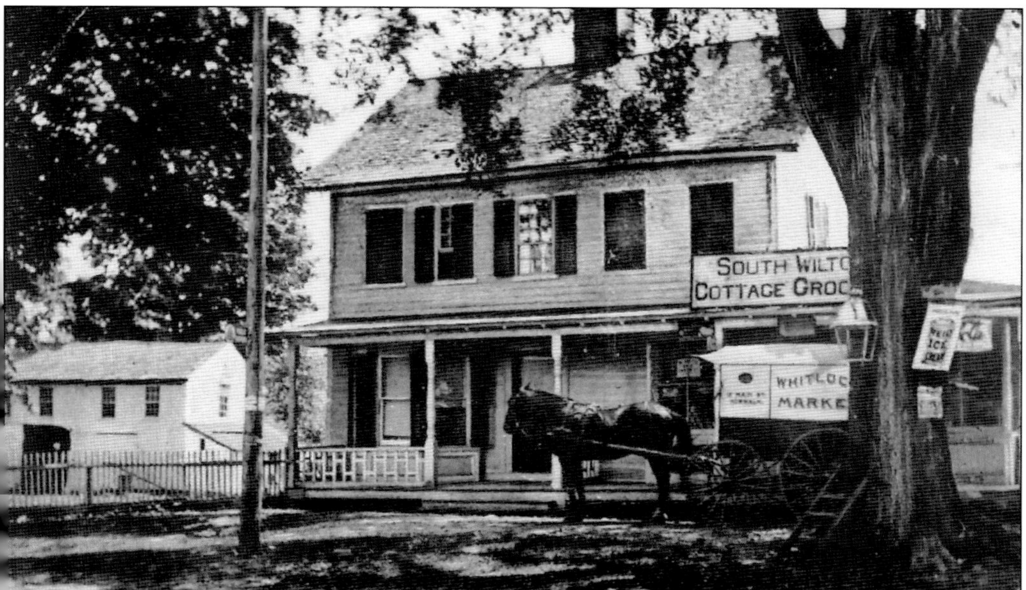

This store, owned by Ignatz Kuehnel, was located south of Kensett Avenue. Note the Whitlock Market wagon in front, which delivered from the market on Main Street, Norwalk. This building once housed Aladdin's Lamp House and has since been torn down.

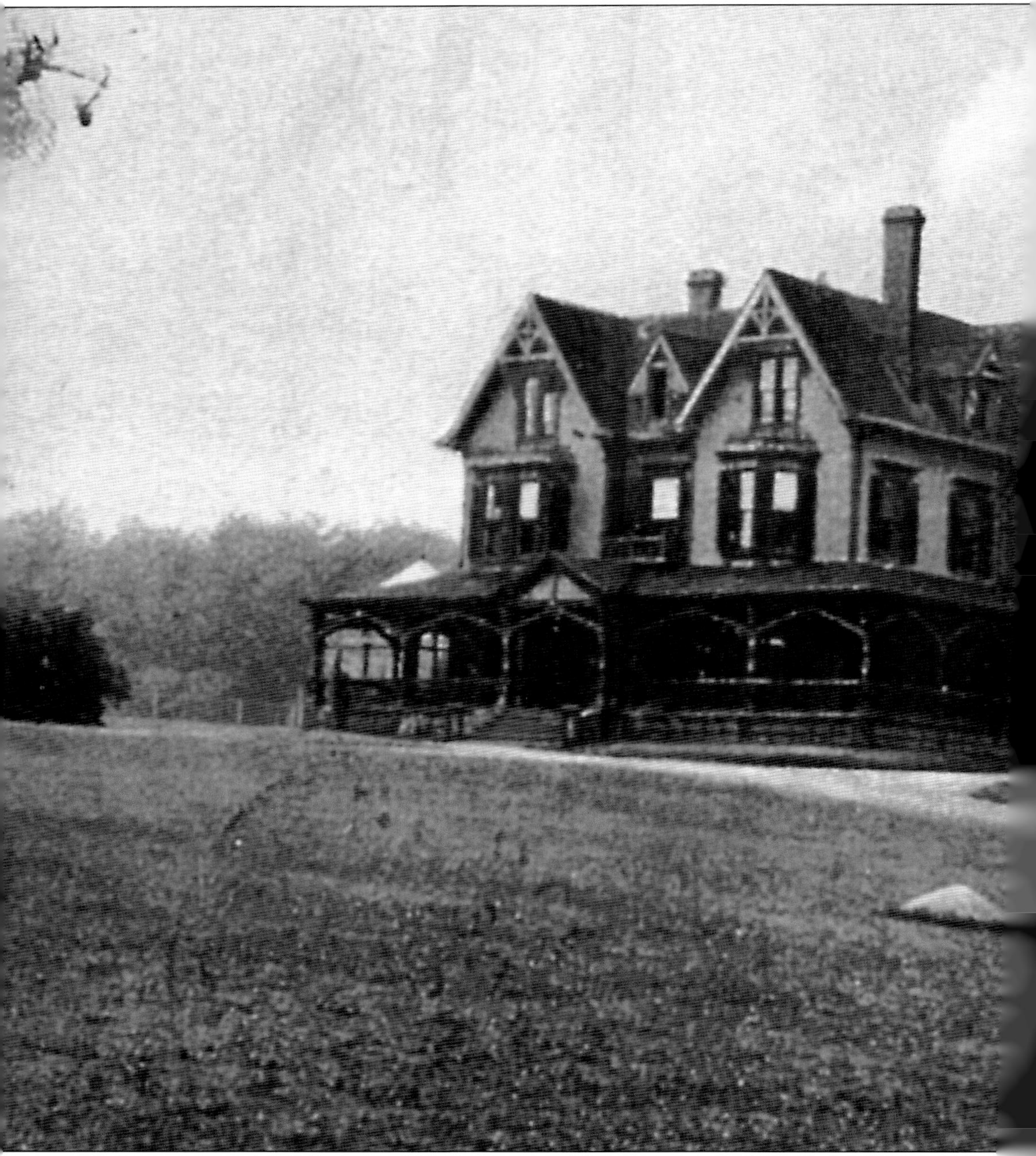

The Kensett Sanitarium, at the junction of Grumman Hill Road and Kensett Avenue, was run by Dr. E.E. Smith, according to F.C. Ogden, Wilton historian. The nature of the patients'

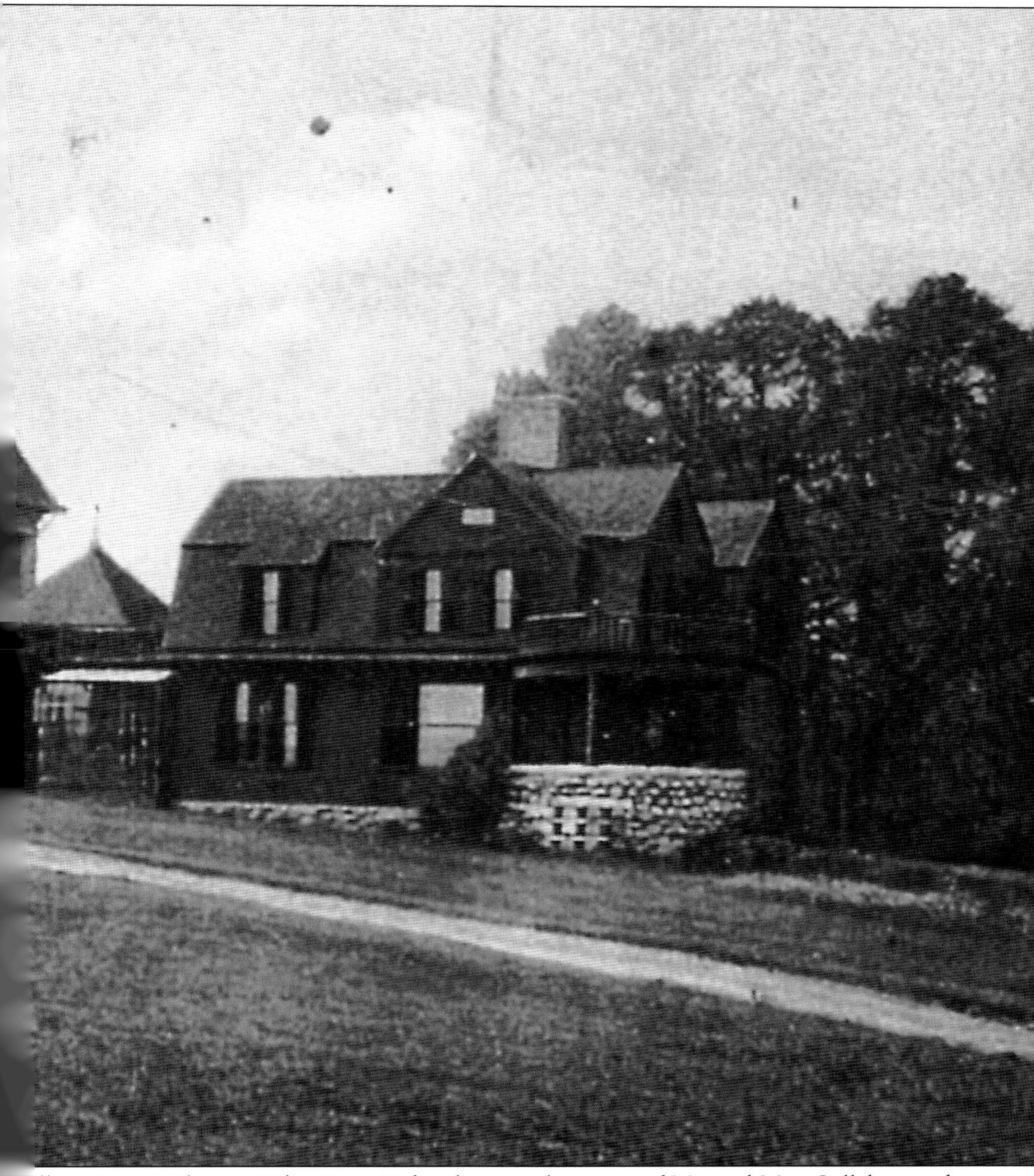

illnesses is not known. The property first became the estate of Mr. and Mrs. Gallaher, and then Cranbury Park.

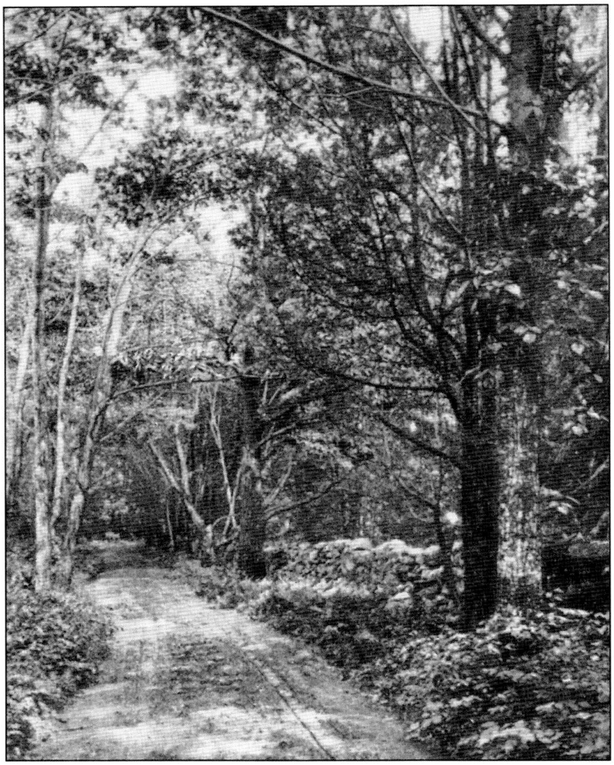

This picturesque approach to the Kensett Sanitarium was paved long ago. The card is a lithochrome print by the American News Co.

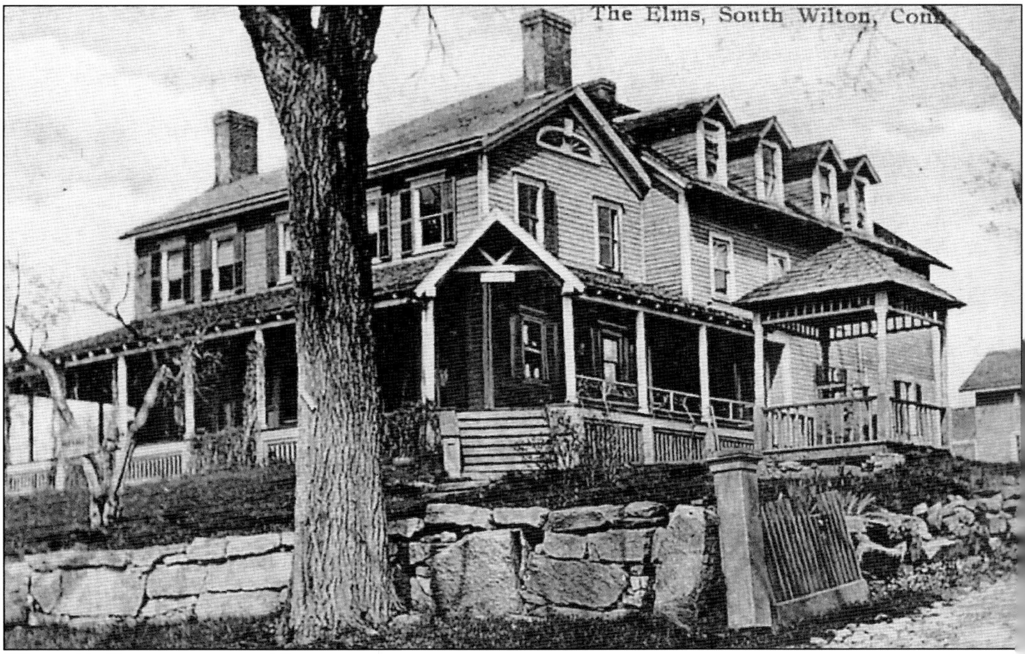

This large house was later run as a nursing home, called Green Meadows, by the Becker family and it was located just south of Wilton Acres on Danbury Road.

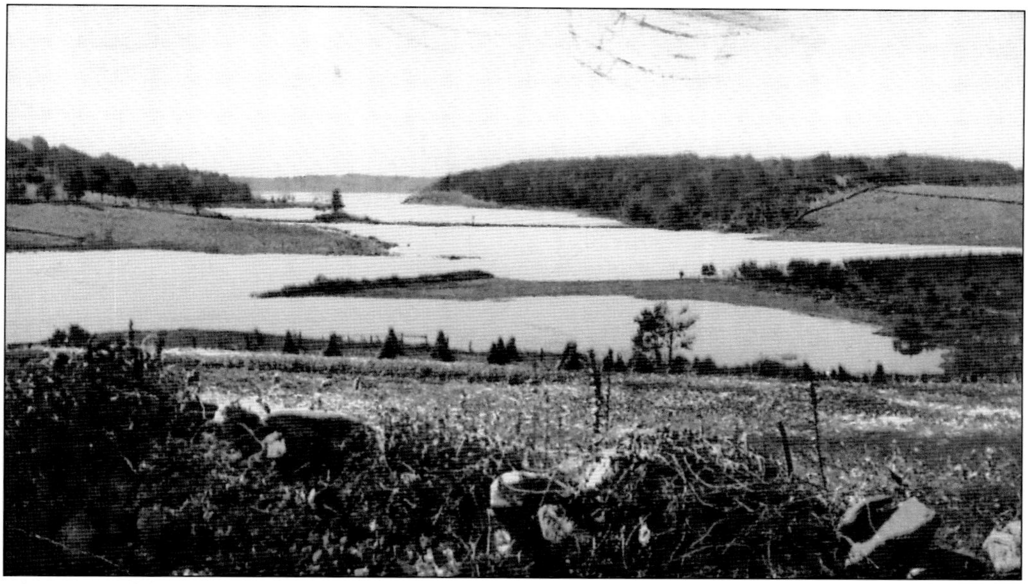

This view of the reservoir from Drum Hill is nicely colored, made in Germany, and published by John T. Hayes, a Norwalk real estate and insurance man. The card is postmarked 1911.

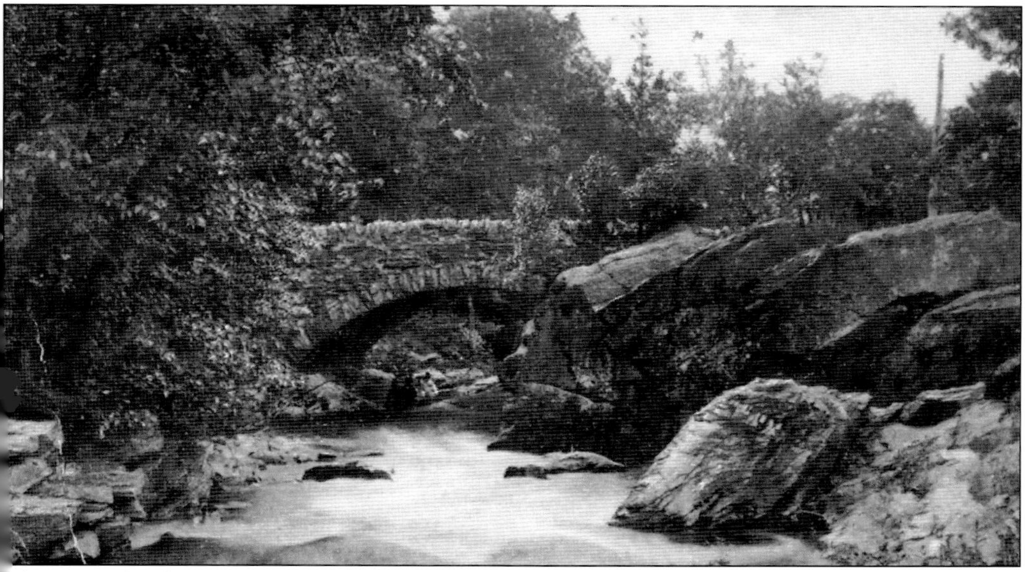

This stone bridge, once the site of daredevil diving, is said to have been covered over by the new Route 7 interchange.

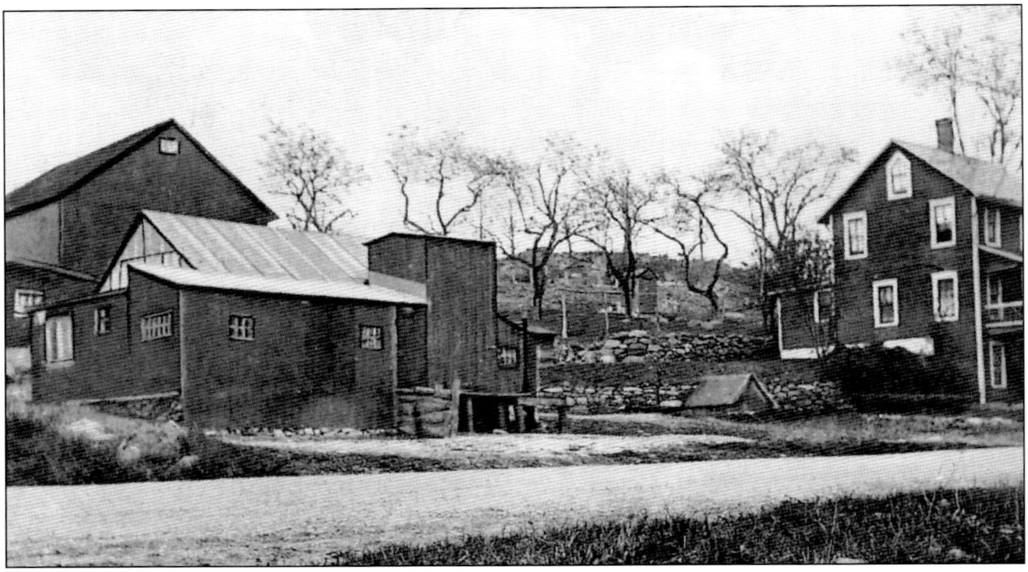

The size of this establishment is an indication of the importance of cider in rural New England. The beverage was an adjunct to almost every undertaking.

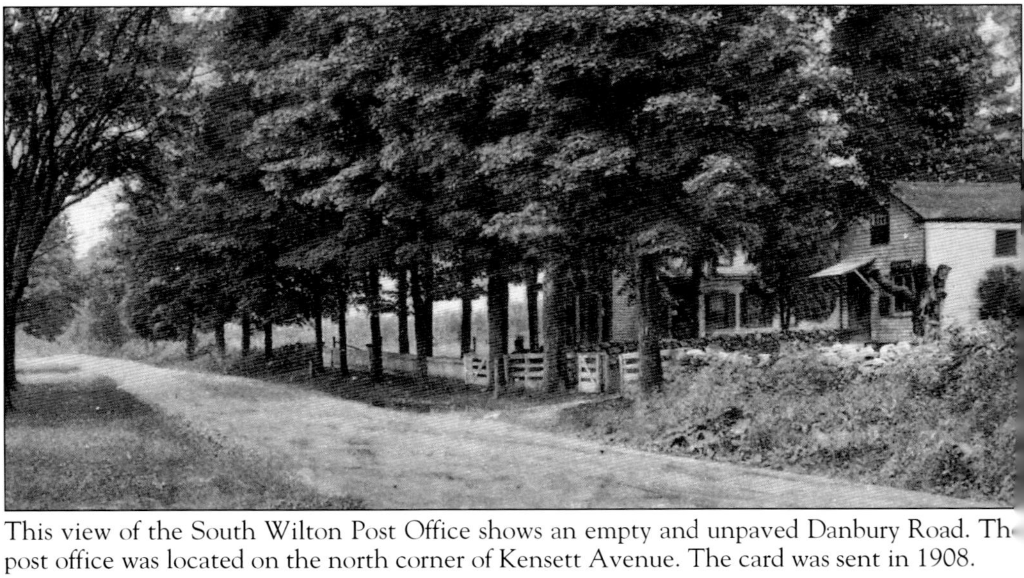

This view of the South Wilton Post Office shows an empty and unpaved Danbury Road. The post office was located on the north corner of Kensett Avenue. The card was sent in 1908.

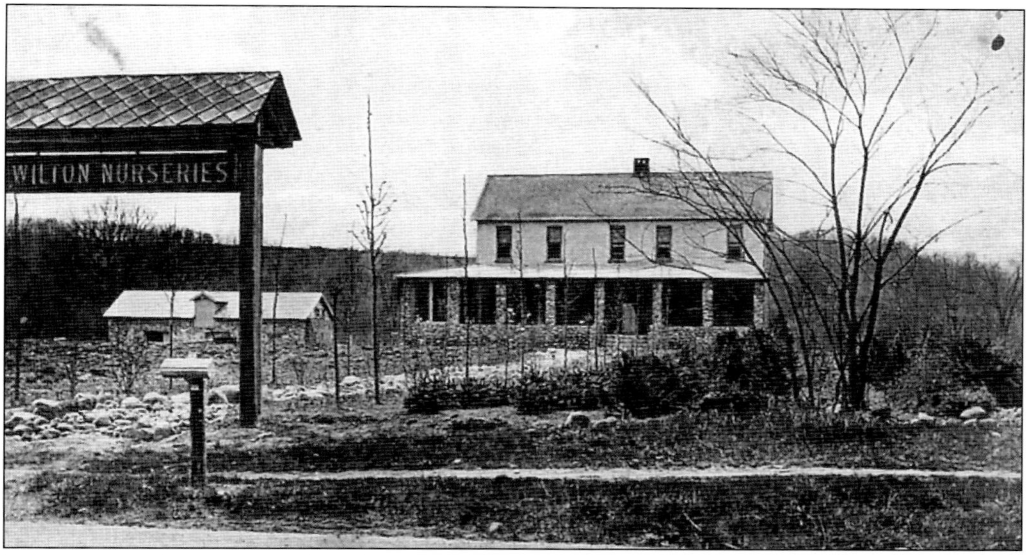

Ignatz Kuehnel photographed and published several cards of this area, sending them to Germany for printing using a method that had been developed there after World War I. Kuehnel published two views of the South Wilton Nurseries. This one features the west side of Danbury Road, where the nursery was started.

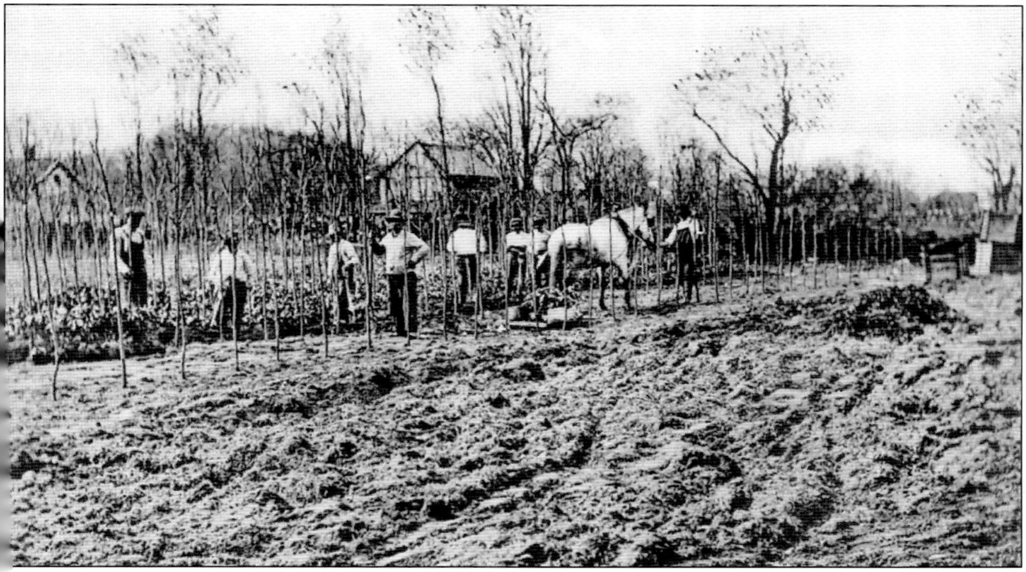

Here is the view on the east side of Danbury Road, where the current Perkin-Elmer building is located. Jacob Van Heiningen, who started the nursery, came from Holland and contributed much to horticulture. He developed the Wilton Juniper.

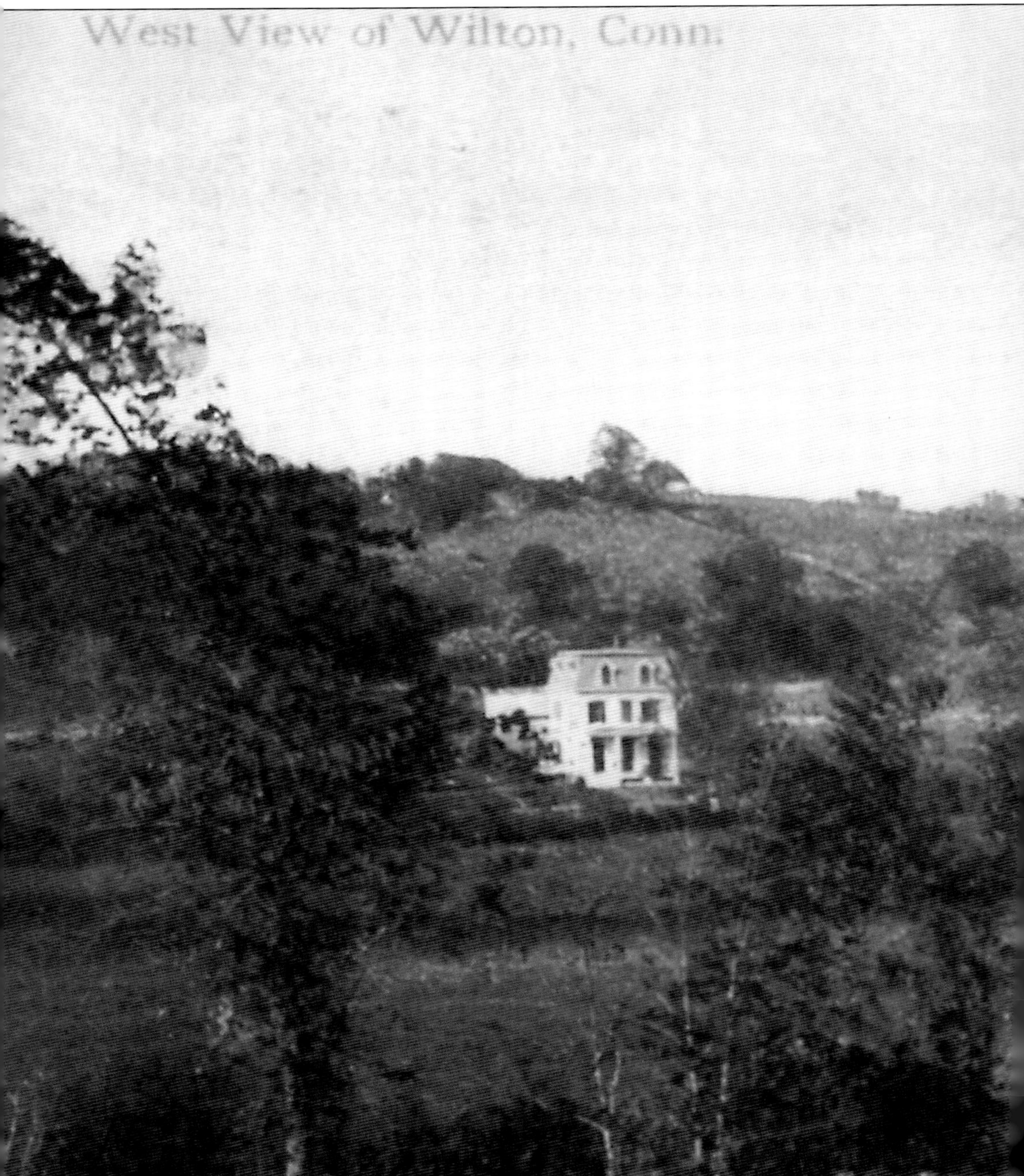

Overlooking Wilton Center from the hill above Danbury Road, this card shows the forme home of Dr. and Mrs. Gorham. The site is now the parking lot of the library. H.G. Thomson'

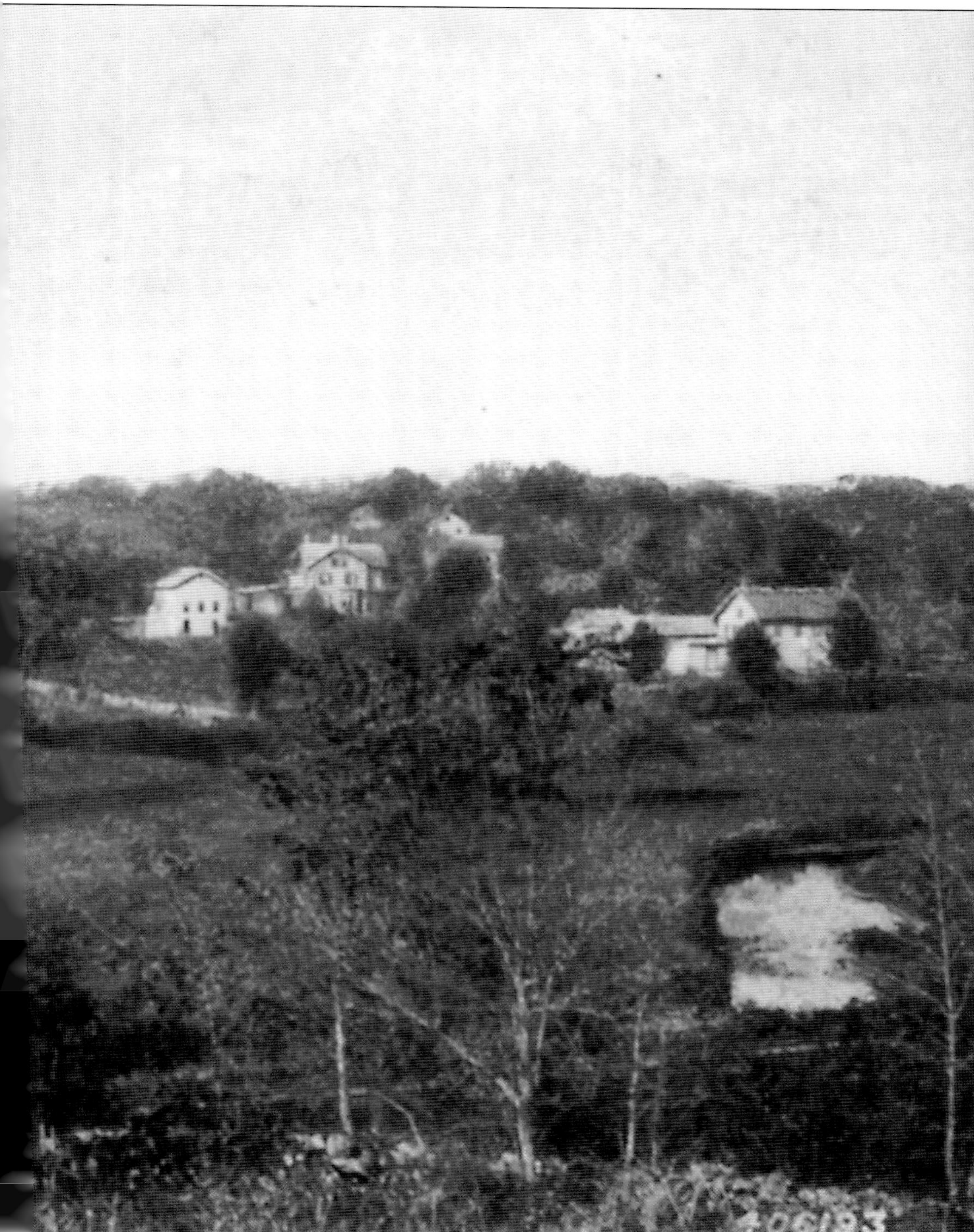

home, turned into the Wilton Arms apartments for returning World War II veterans by G.E. Hubbard, is visible to the right.

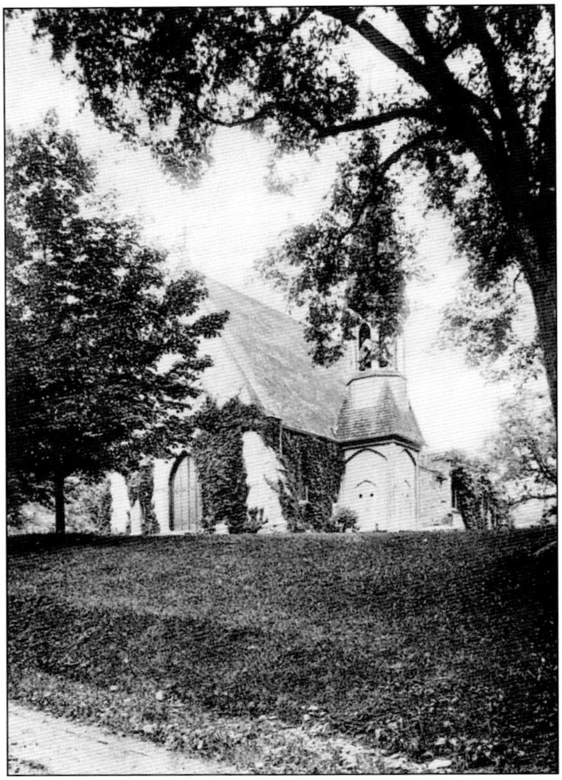

Another contender in the postcard field, Mrs. E.F. Davies had this view of St. Matthew's published. She was an early postmistress at the South Wilton Post Office, according to a U.S. Post Office listing.

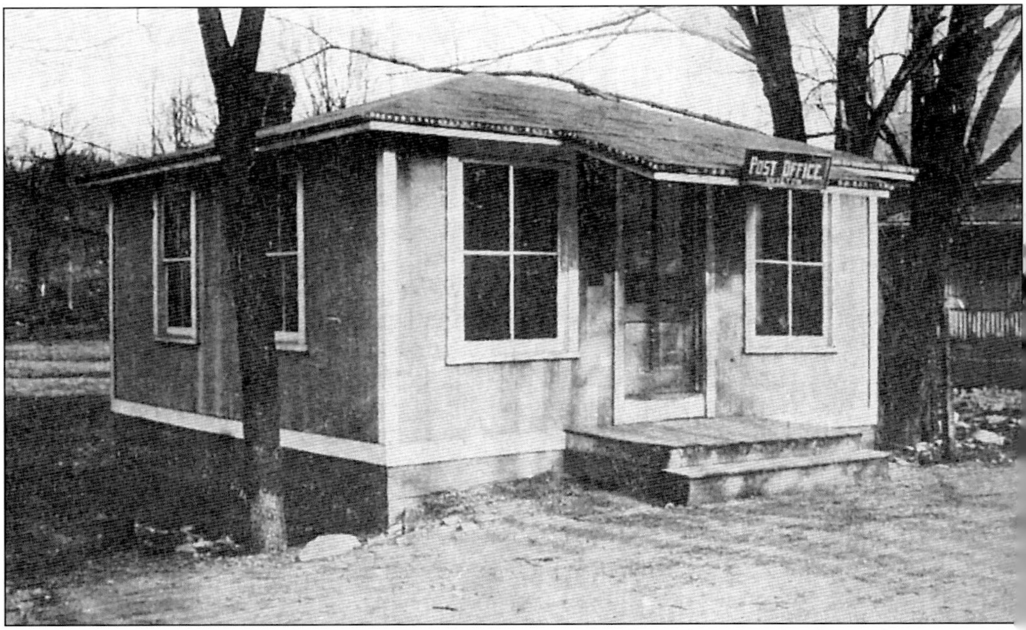

This post office on the town green was probably the building that caught fire. This particula fire was spotted by Florence Godfrey Holly, who lived in the old Burlock (Charles Dana) hous with her grandparents.

Three

Mixed Methods: Local and National

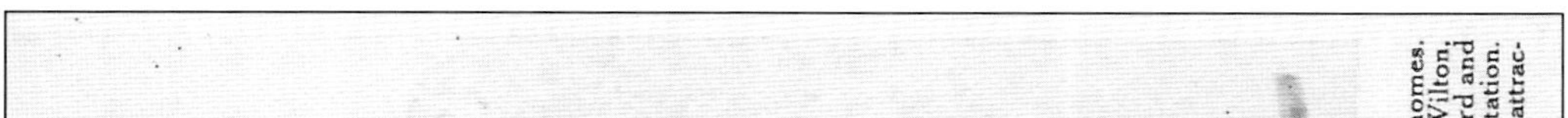

The inscription on this card reads: "Wilton, Conn., an historic town with many colonial homes. Named by the first settlers in memory of their home town in Wilton, England. It is situated on the Danbury division of the Hartford and New Haven R. R., and is 48 miles from the Grand Central Station. Among rolling hills and fertile valleys, it is one of the most attractive towns in Fairfield County."

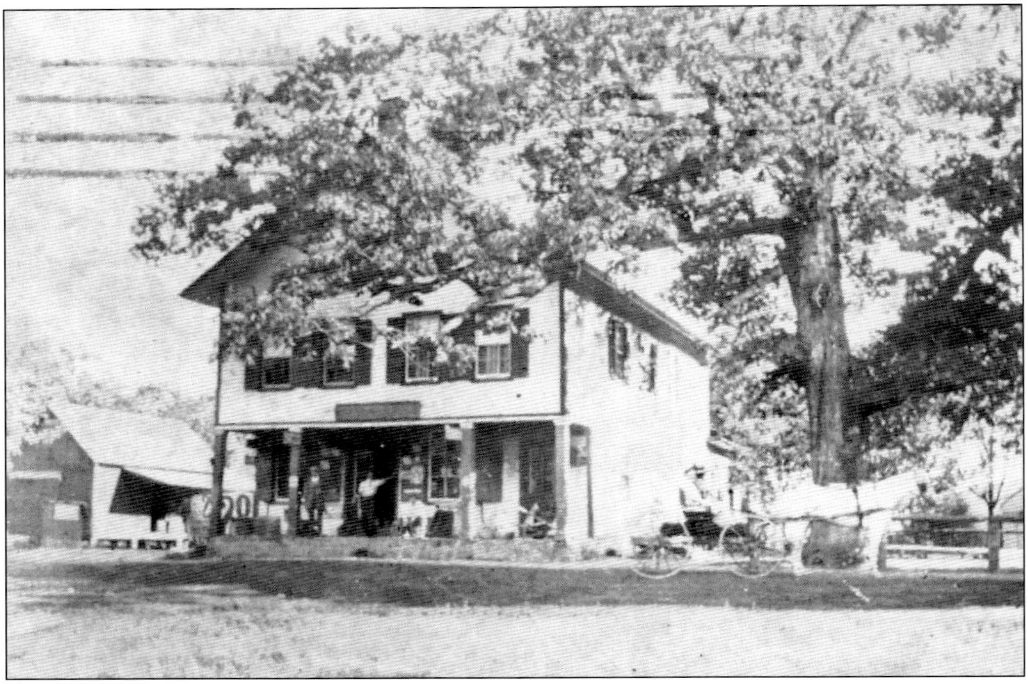

This building was erected in 1802 and was originally the first Episcopal church in Wilton. In 1862 it was purchased and removed to its present site. The structure was remodeled and has served as a leading store in Wilton.

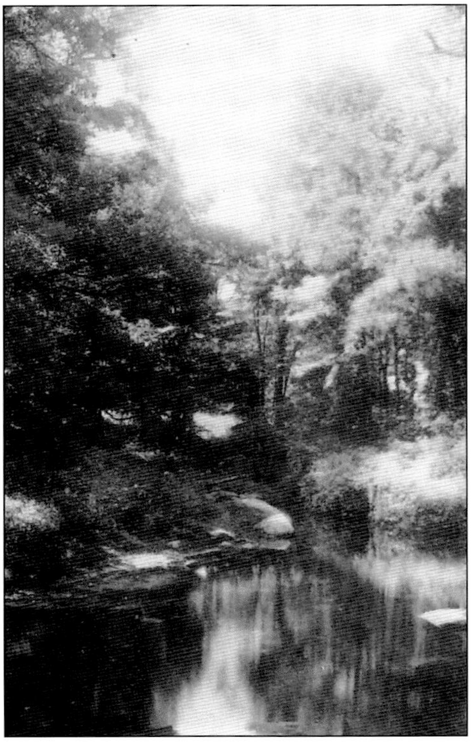

The Nomis Manufacturing Co. made many sepia-tinted cards of Wilton scenes, including some of Orem's Field and Shady Nook. This card was given to the authors by Mrs. Miriam Northrup Saunders.

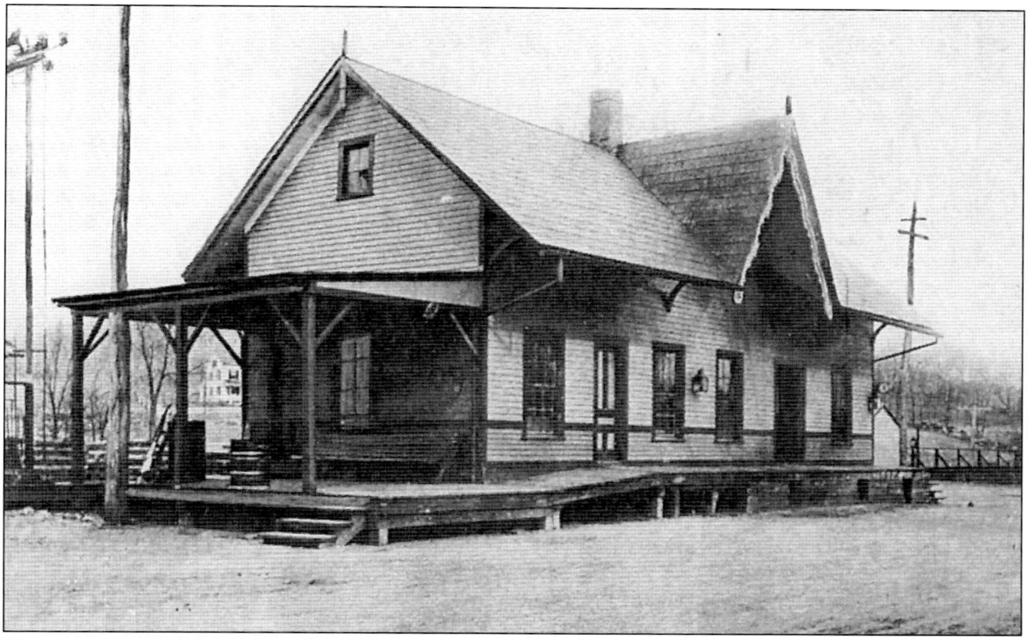

Here is a view of the railroad station taken from the north on the river side. It shows the stately home of Mr. and Mrs. St. John Comstock on Danbury Road in the background.

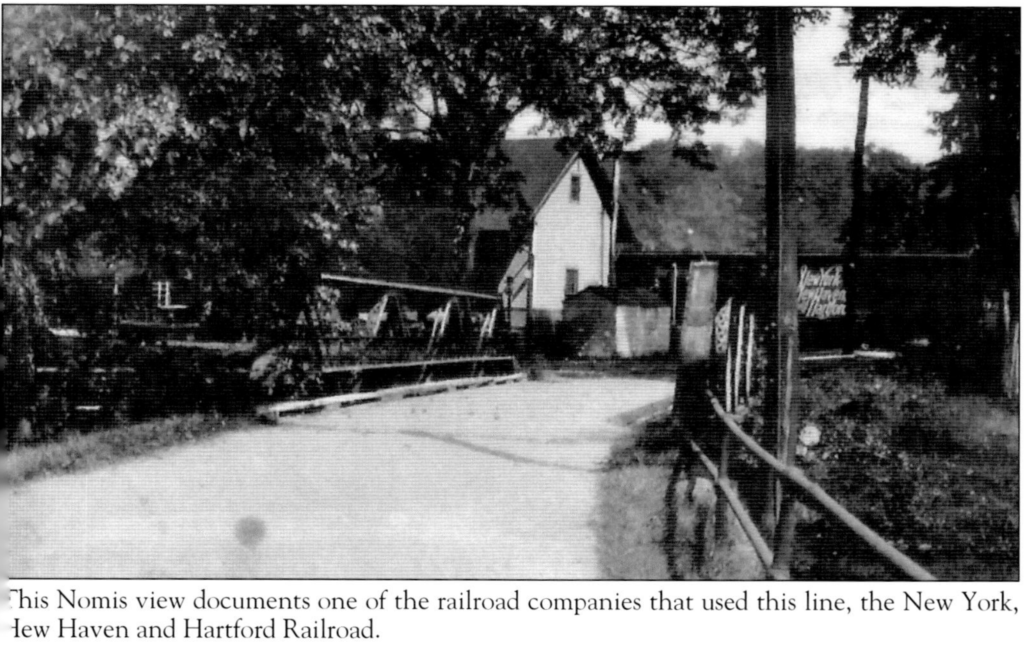

This Nomis view documents one of the railroad companies that used this line, the New York, New Haven and Hartford Railroad.

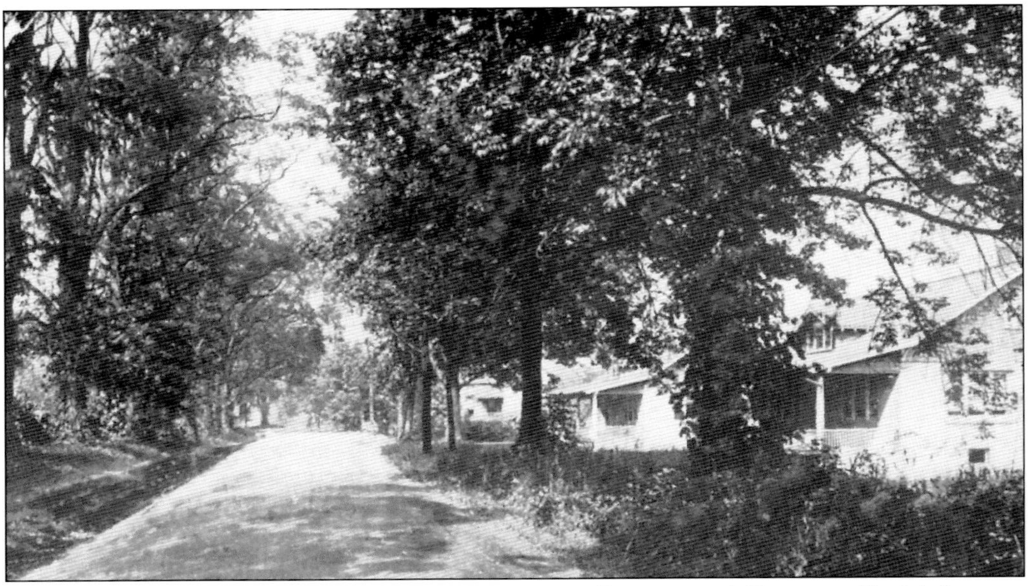

Cottages and Carpenter Gothic houses lined the southern part of Center Street. These cottages occupied the area of the Gregory and Adams law offices and the parking lot.

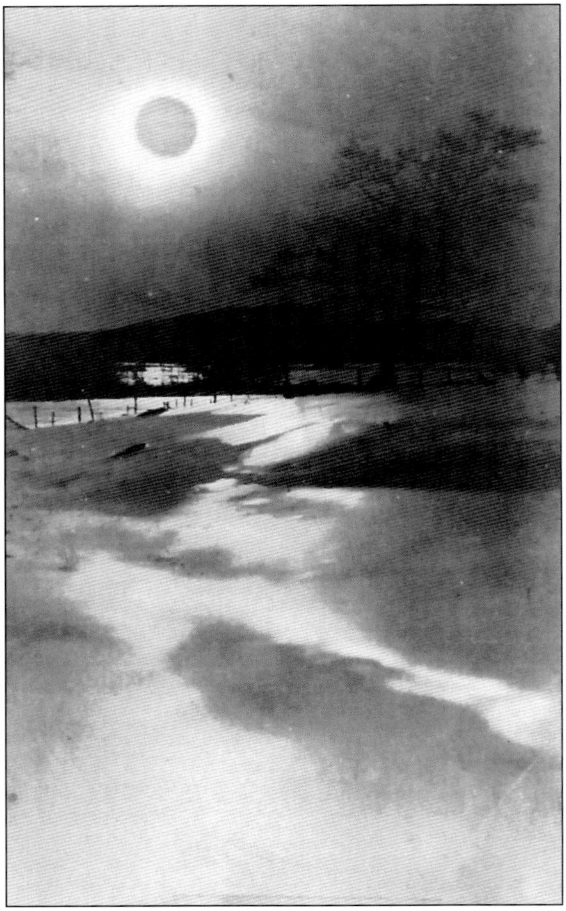

This may be an early attempt at night photography, or, as Rita C.S. Sturges suggested, an attempt at recording an eclipse. The only sure thing is that the photograph was taken in winter.

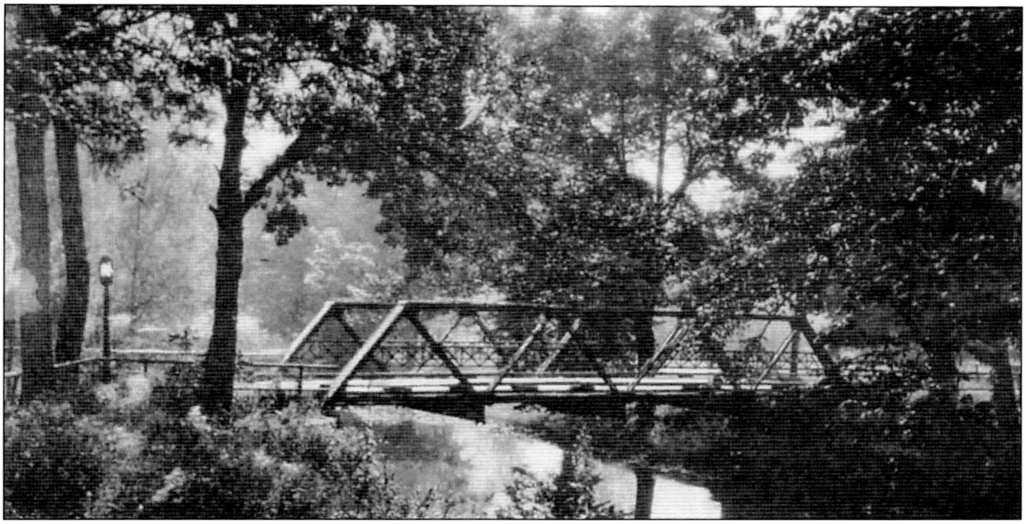

This steel bridge evidences the fact that, even by 1905, this type of construction had apparently replaced the wooden style so often used in Wilton. A early form of street lighting is also visible.

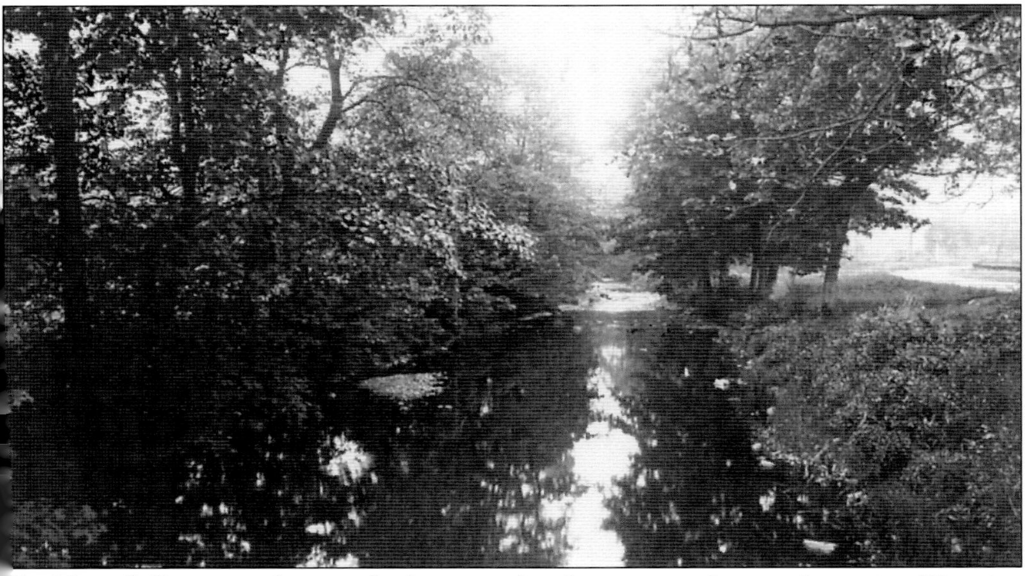

The Norwalk River was photographed near a railroad crossing, perhaps at the station. The view was published on a card by Underwood and Underwood.

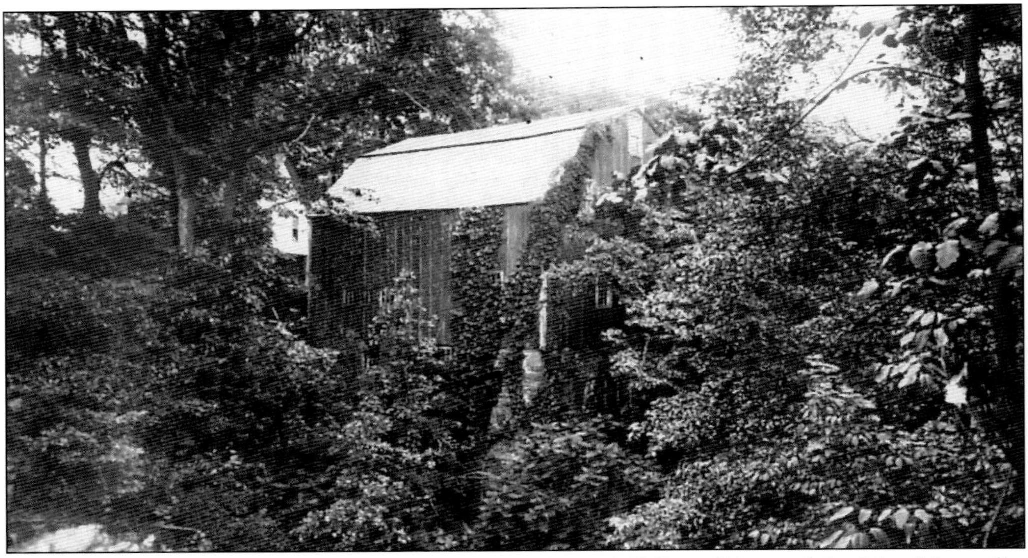

The old mill building on Lovers' Lane sat next to Merwin's Falls well beyond the life of the mill.

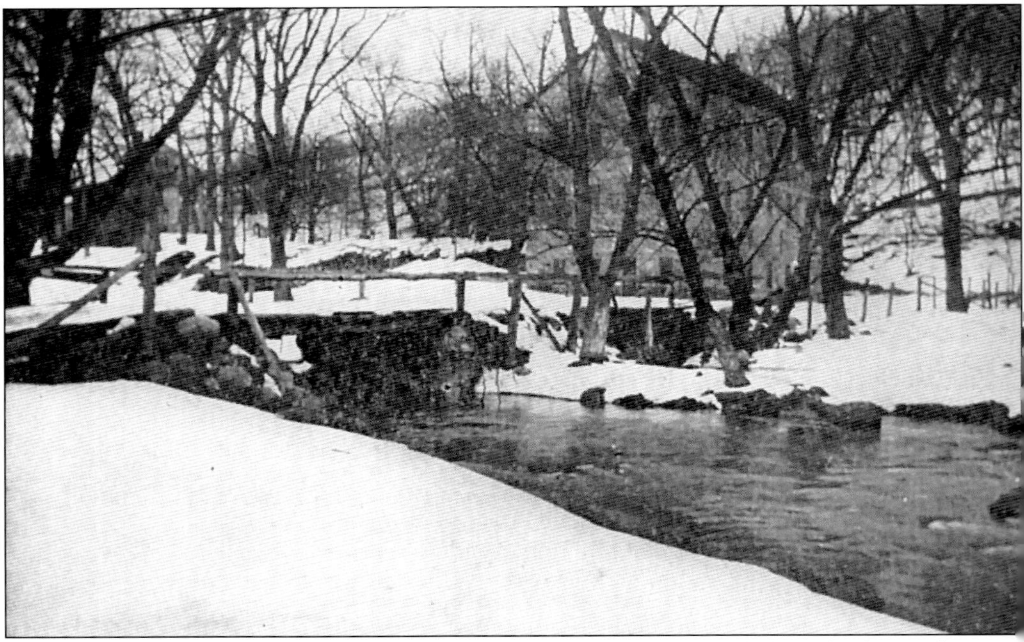

The old gristmill in Georgetown has also been a woolen mill and the Glenberg Chemica Works, which processed herbs and spices for medicinal purposes. Some of the old stones fron the mill were used to construct the Stone Mill Market nearby.

This postcard of the Congregational church was made when the horse sheds—essential features of early churches—a small parish hall, and the three small houses of the Davenport, Middlebrook, and Thayer families nestled around the sanctuary.

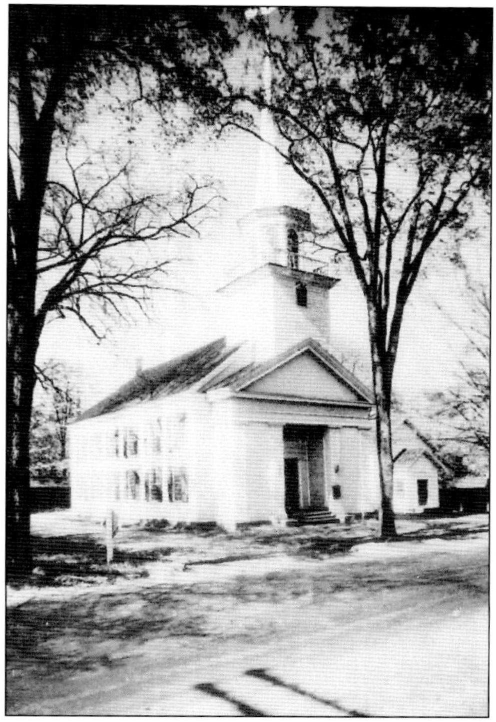

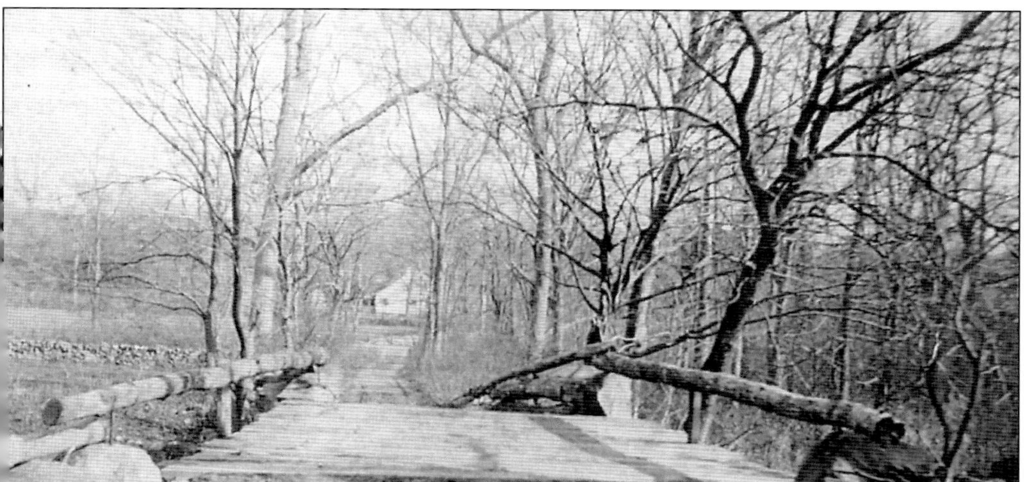

.overs' Lane and the bridge at its foot once led to the railroad station and old Danbury Road.

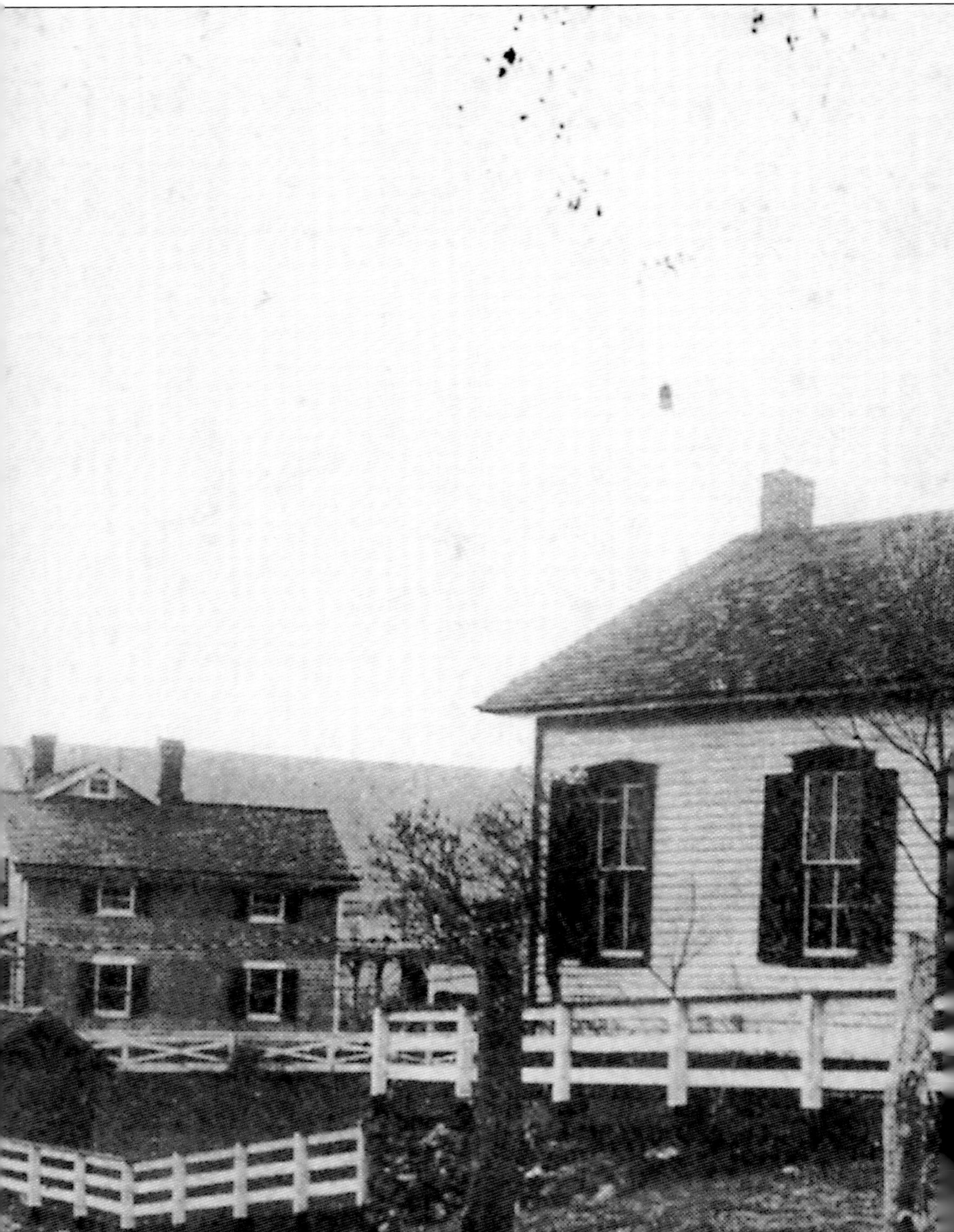

The District Number 7 Cannondale School, once on the corner of Olmstead Hill Road an

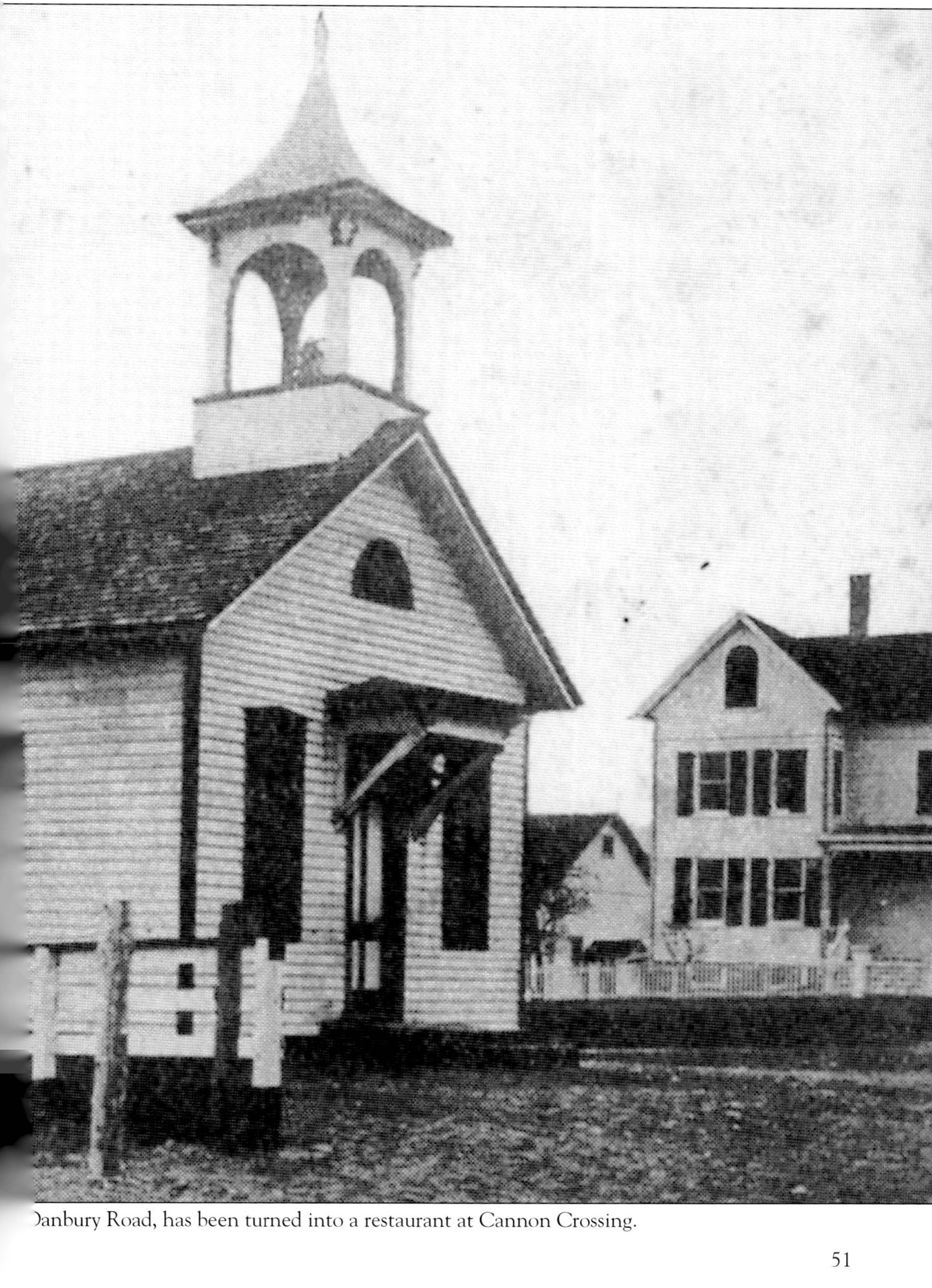

)anbury Road, has been turned into a restaurant at Cannon Crossing.

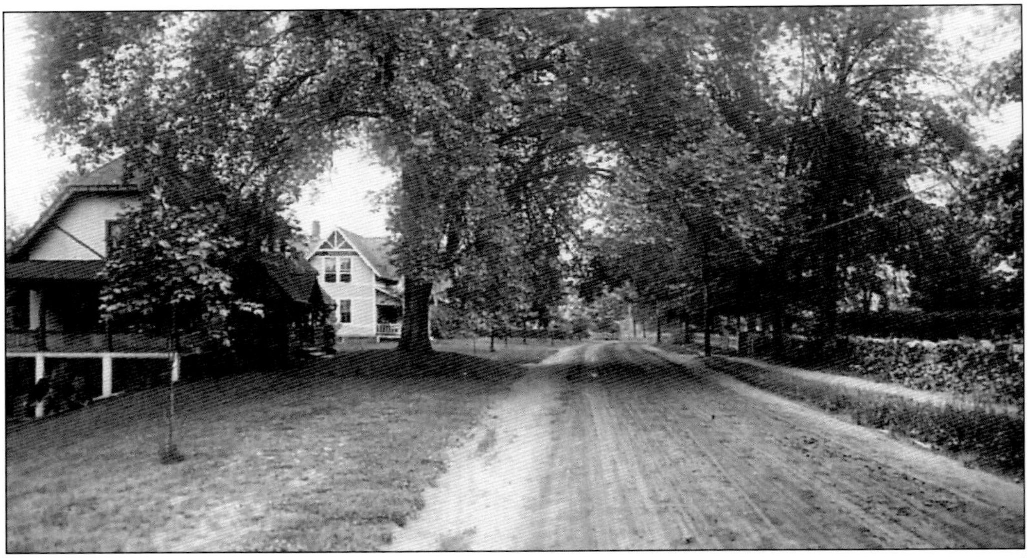

This view of Cottage Row was taken from the north. It shows an unpaved street and probably the only existing building (seen on the left in the foreground) in the area. It was the telephone exchange in the days of the party line.

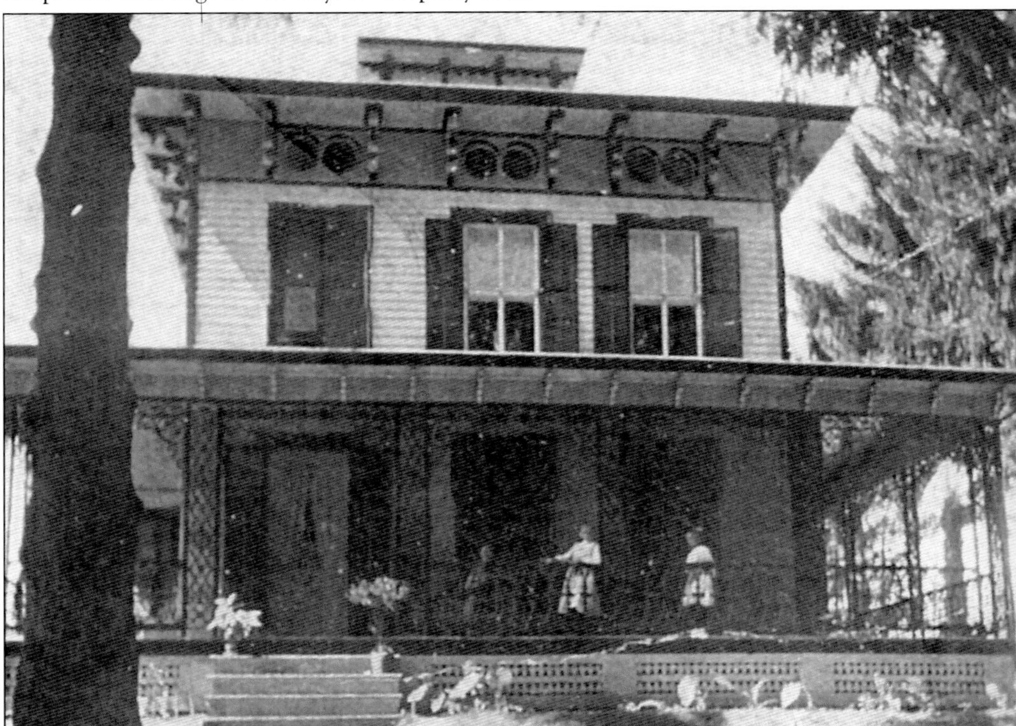

This was once the home of Dr. J. Edward Turner, whose grave was commemorated by the American Medical Society for his work with alcoholism. The beautiful Italianate building, located on Ridgefield Road, has since been a guesthouse and then home to three generations of Schlichtings.

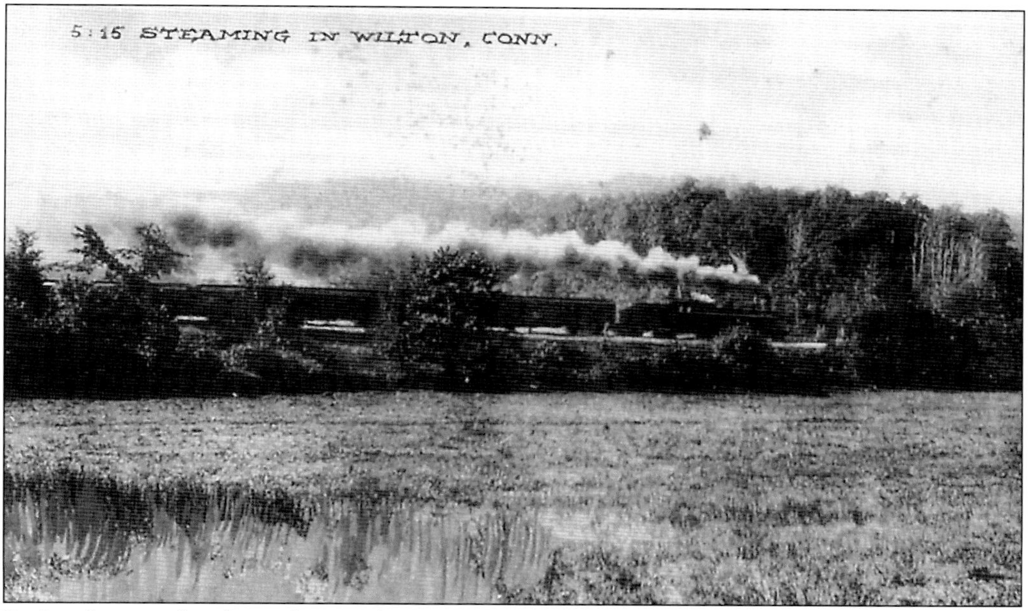

Railroading in the days of steam has a romantic aura. A deed in Wilton's property records provides for water to be supplied to the old steam engines, but by 1924, *The Norwalk Hour* indicated that electrification was imminent. However, self-propelled diesel Budd cars eventually came into use before electrification was achieved.

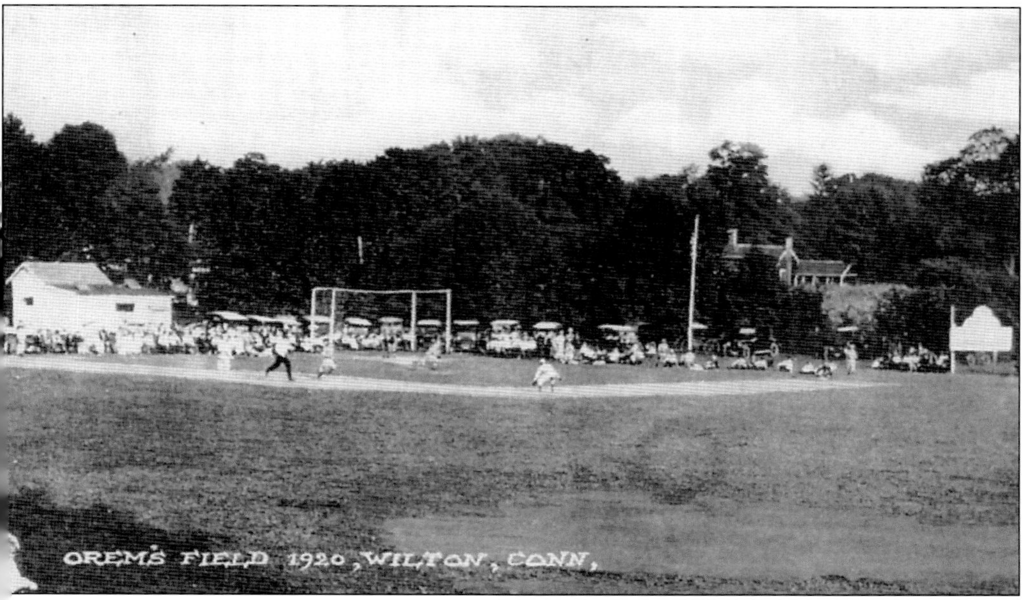

Charles Orem ran a dairy and started a baseball field and a refreshment stand where he sold baked goods made by local women. He also sold and developed what is now known as Orem's Lane.

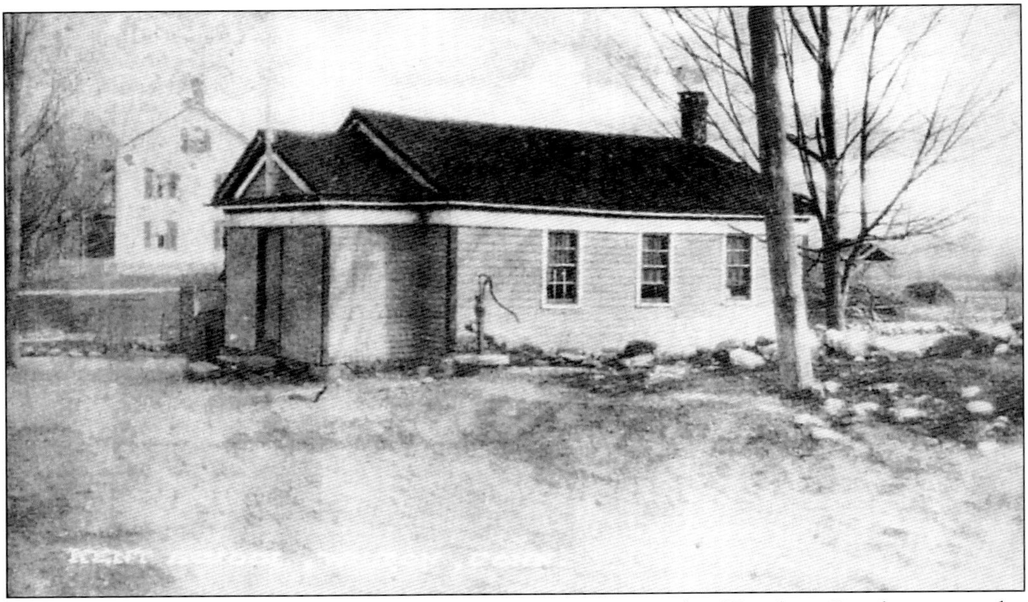

The District Number 6 Kent School was located on the west side of Danbury Road opposite the junction with the Westport Road. It was built in 1843 and was used as a one-room schoolhouse until the new Center School was opened in the late 1920s. It was later used by the rural branch of the Norwalk YMCA, then the Wilton Athletic Club. The former Rockwell farmhouse can be seen to the south; that was where pupils went for pails of water.

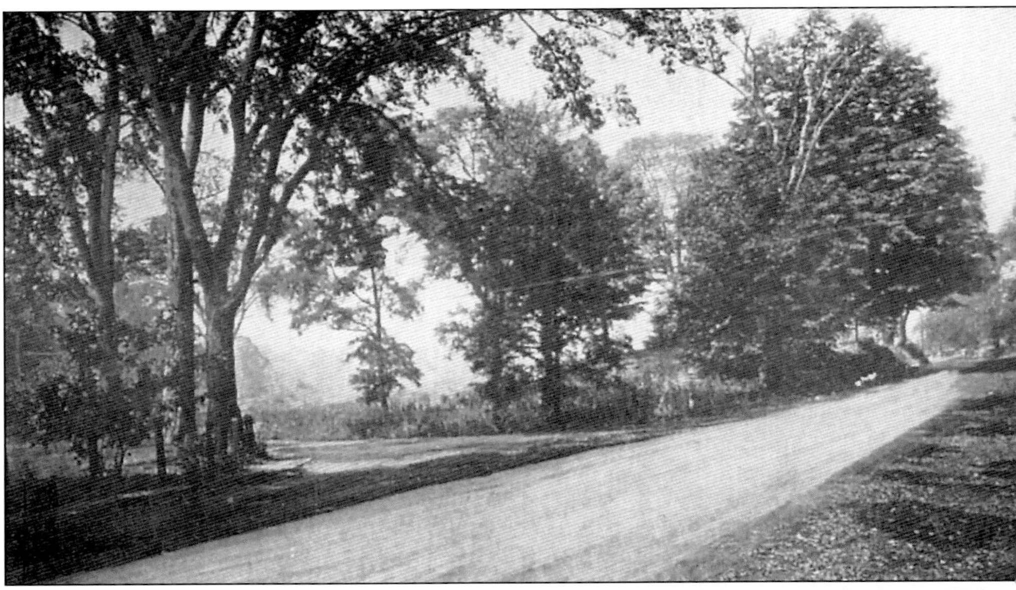

This road crossed the railroad tracks past Jessie's Gas Station and then over a bridge to Wilton Center. Jessie's Gas Station was commemorated in a painting by Richard Daggy. Jessie was a maiden lady perhaps ahead of her time.

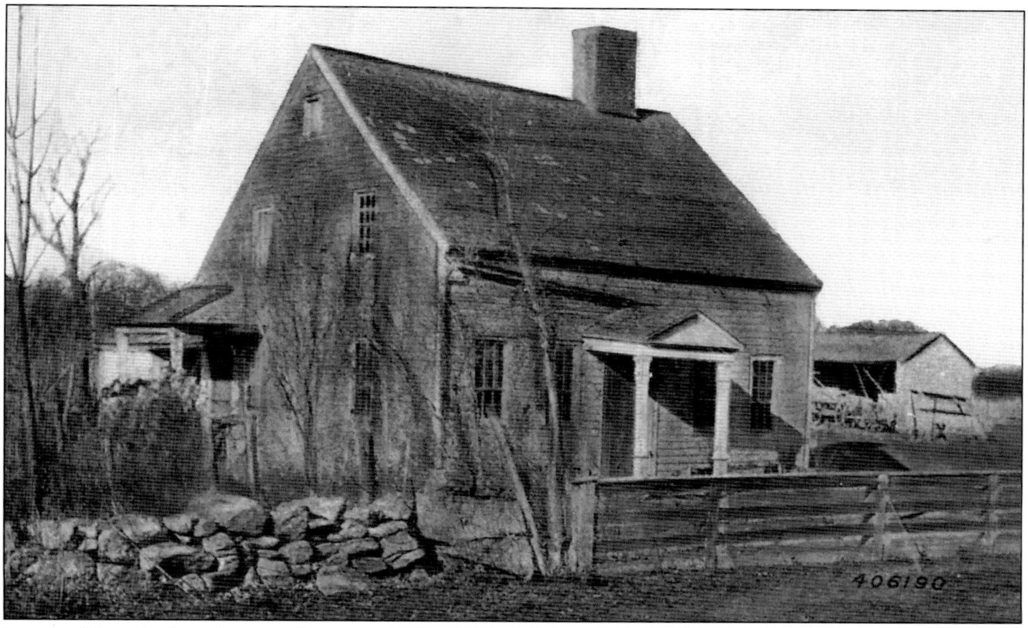

Many Church family members moved to Canada, and Daniel Church left this house to his parents. The home was located on the west side of Danbury Road, near where Westport Road enters Wilton.

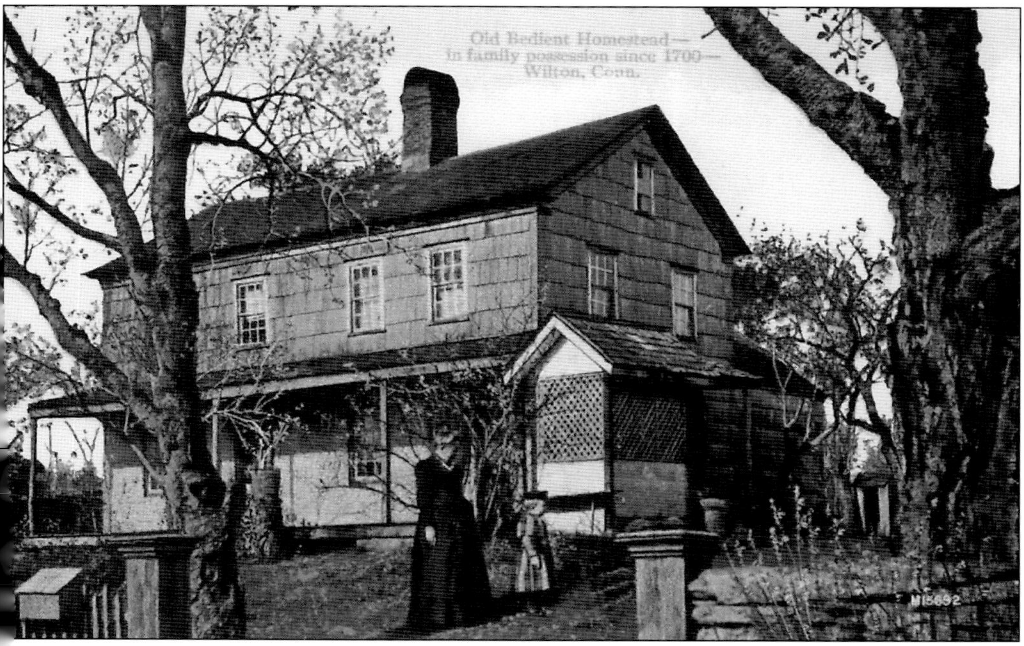

The Bedients were a large family with many pieces of property and many family connections in the Sharp Hill-Hurlbutt Street area.

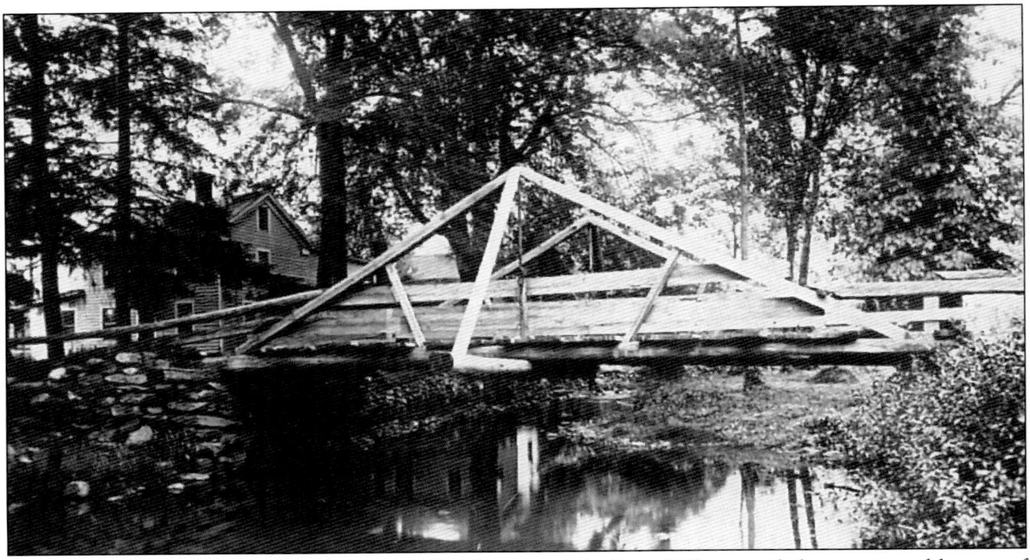

This bridge led to the railroad station, the Cannondale Post Office, and the store and home of the Ralph Gregory family.

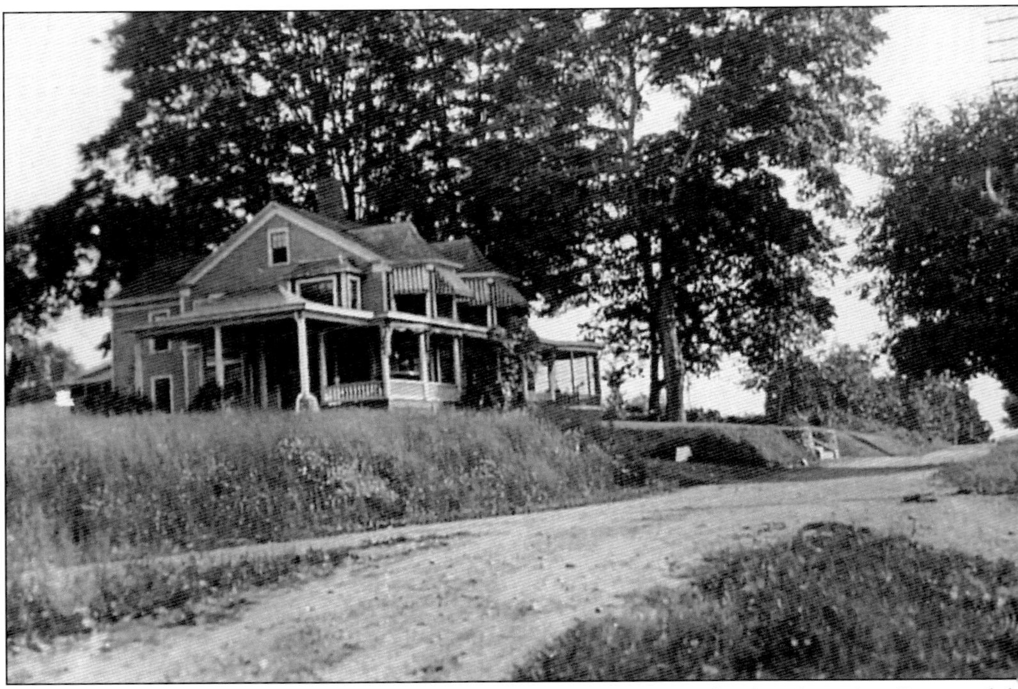

Jan and June Robbins were a husband and wife writing team who lived in the Cannondale section of Wilton. At least one of their articles appeared in a well-known magazine such a *Yankee* or *Reader's Digest* during their residency.

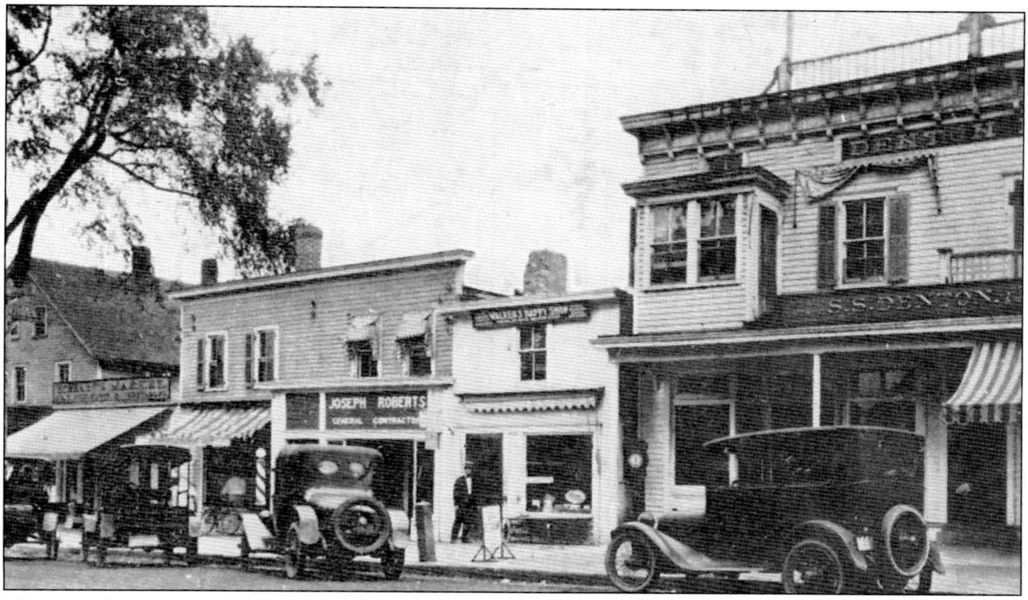

No town's citizens live entirely within the perambulation lines of their town. Supplies, employment, entertainment, or higher education may be found over the border. Ridgefield's main street was developed earlier than Wilton's center.

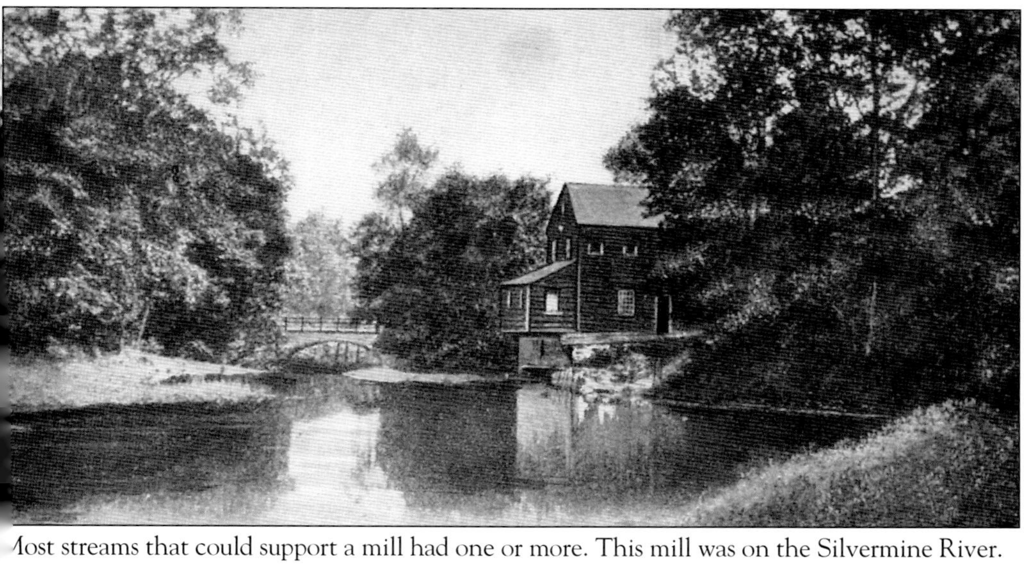

Most streams that could support a mill had one or more. This mill was on the Silvermine River.

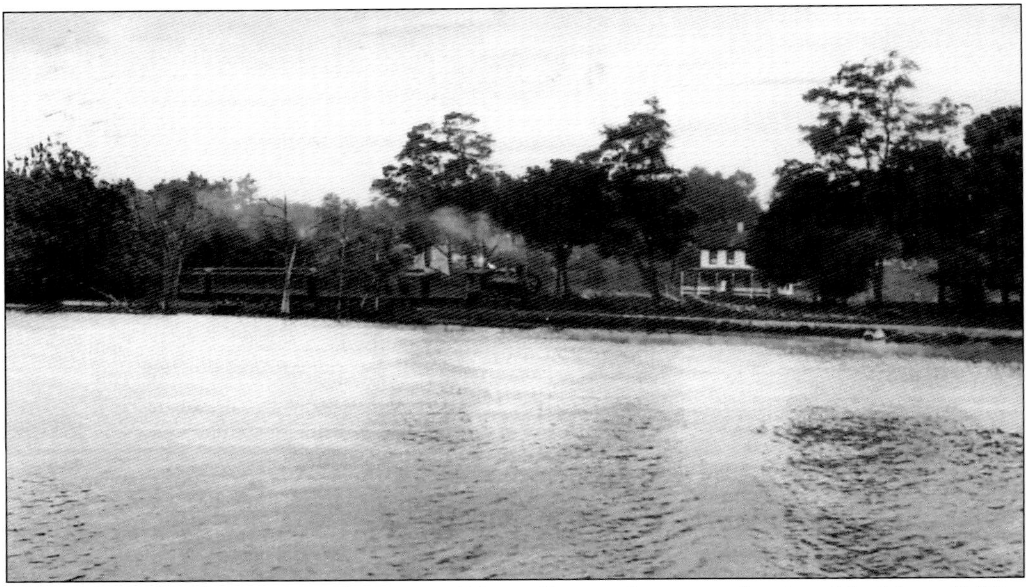

The Mill Pond in the Winnipauk section of Norwalk was adjacent to the site of the Norwalk Tire and Rubber Company and, more recently, the general headquarters of the Caldor Corporation. The pond also followed the route of the railroad line to Wilton.

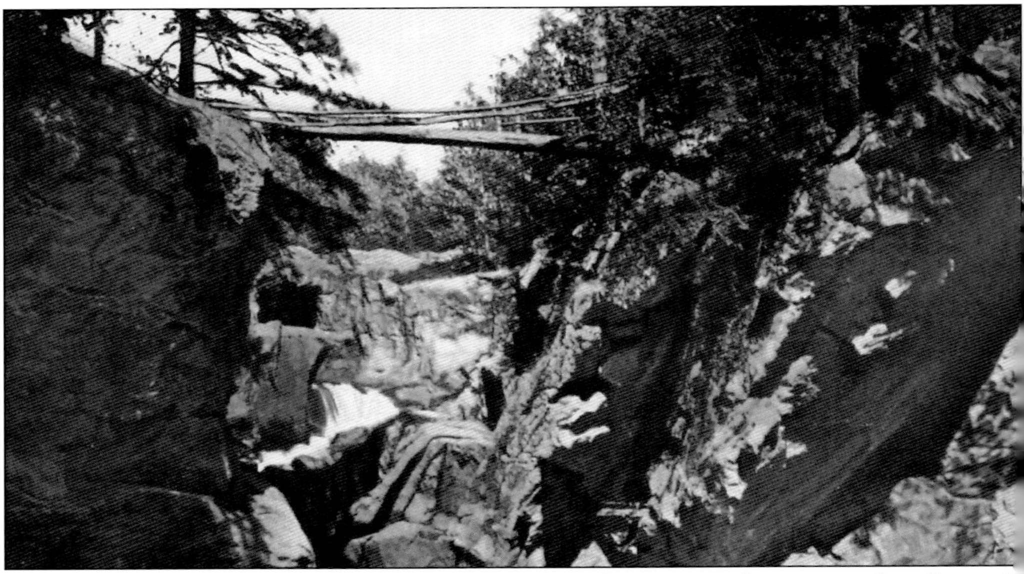

In the valley that divides Wilton and Weston is this stream that powered mills, earl manufactories, and the forge.

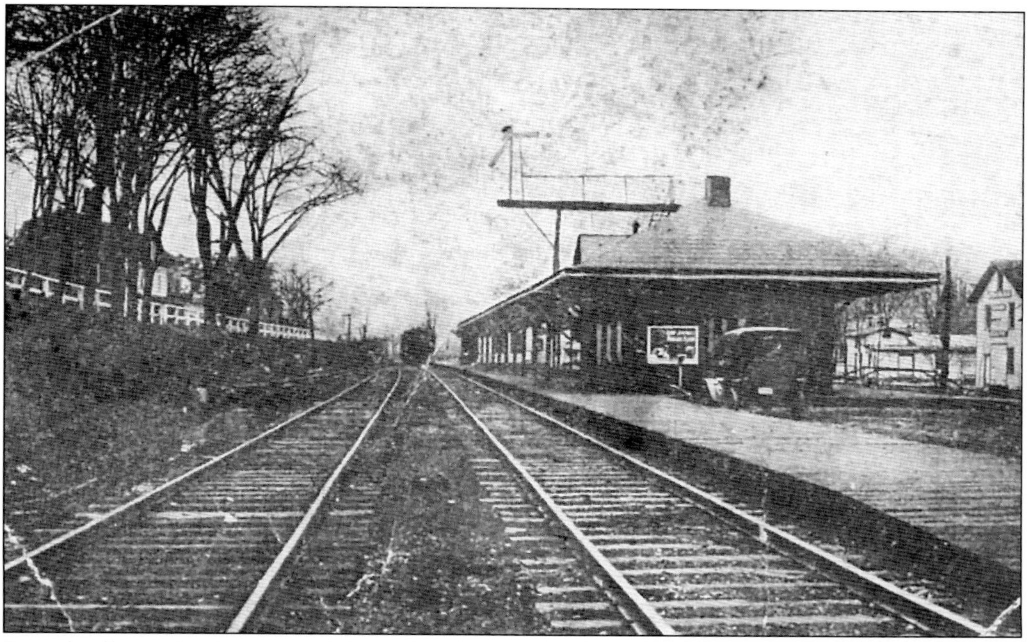

Branchville, at the junction of the railroad line to Ridgefield with the line to Danbury, was an important stop for parts of several surrounding towns.

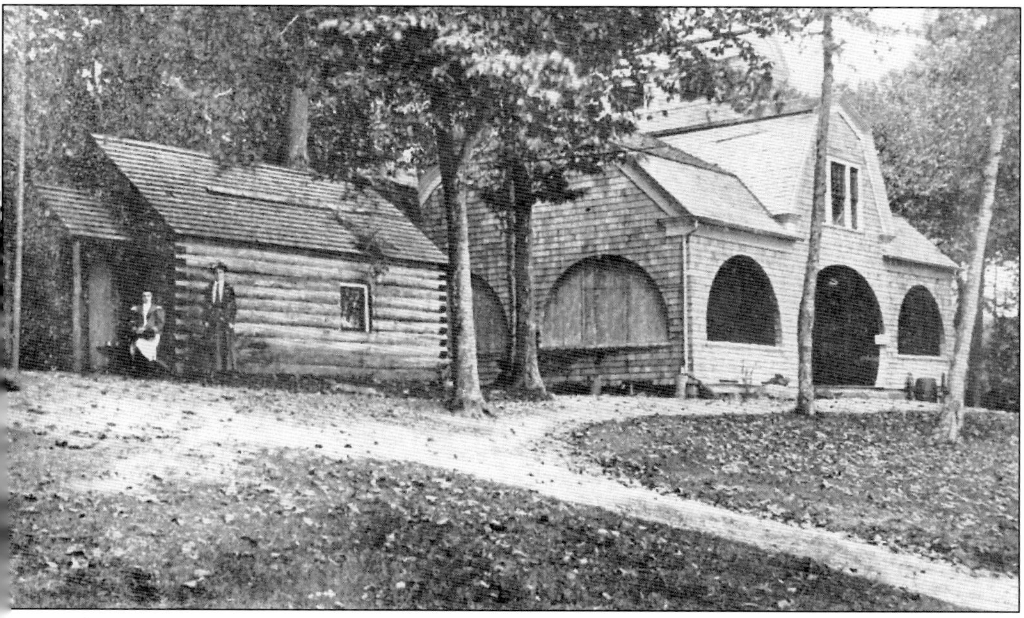

n nearby Redding is this park, commemorating Israel Putnam of Revolutionary fame, where ·ikes, picnics, and family reunions have taken place over the years.

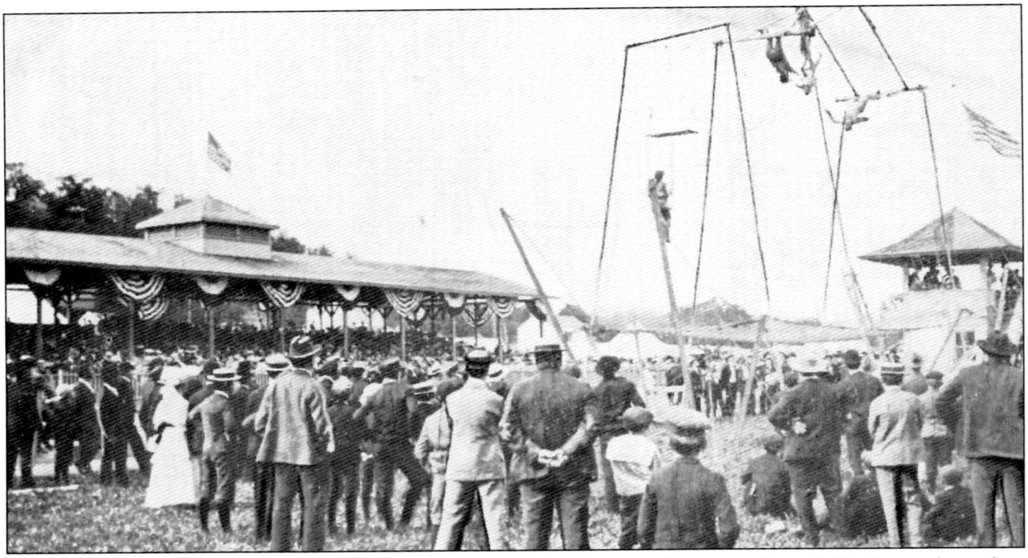

Each year people were drawn to the Great Danbury Fair: to the agricultural displays, the sales, contests, rides, and food.

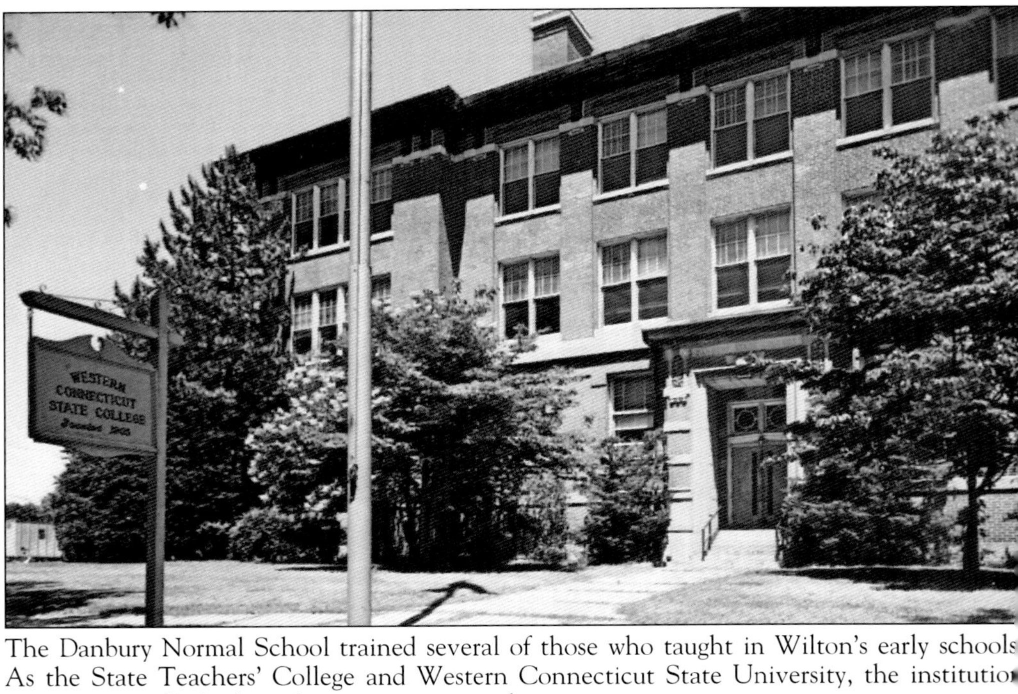

The Danbury Normal School trained several of those who taught in Wilton's early schools As the State Teachers' College and Western Connecticut State University, the institution continues to offer higher education to area students.

Four

Commercialism Comes to Wilton

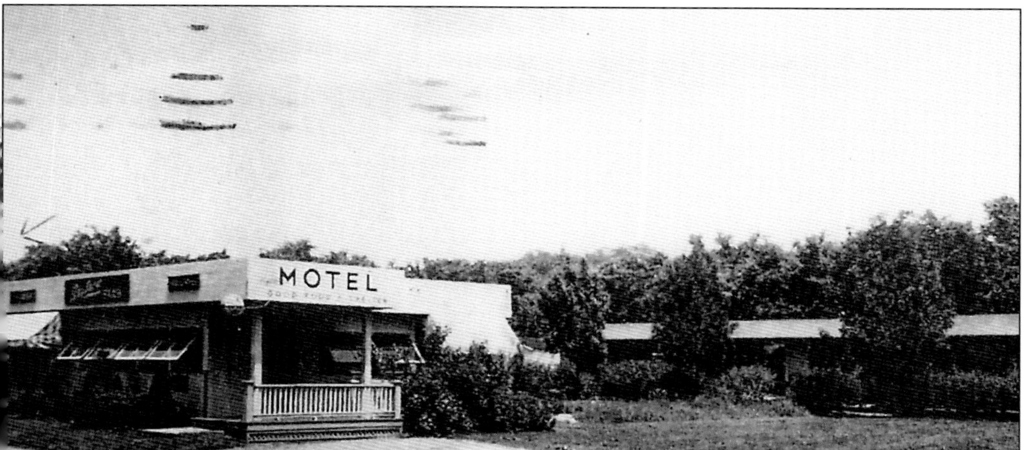

John Disbrow, Milestone Garage owner and early school bus proprietor, also built cabins and a restaurant. The Pepper Pot restaurant is remembered for its large variety of ice cream flavors. This view, captured on the east side of Danbury Road just below Perkin-Elmer, is represented in an original contact print from Dexter Press, from which Silver Craft lithocards were made.

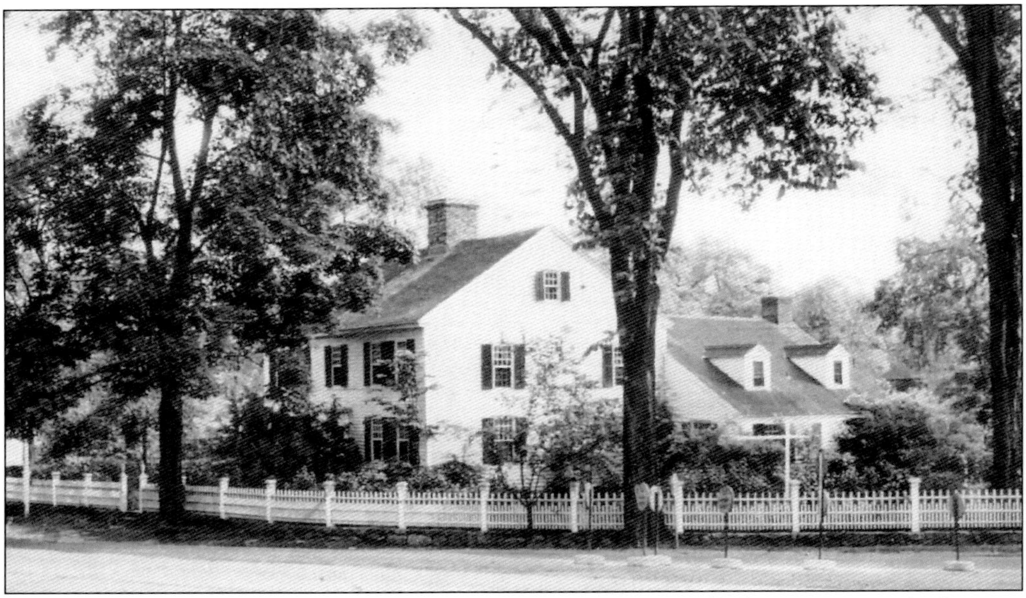

Two ladies, Ms. Allen and Ms. Shaw, ran a tearoom/restaurant called Crossways in the historic Sloane-Raymond-Fitch House across from the stone church. When they moved their restaurant north, the name went with them.

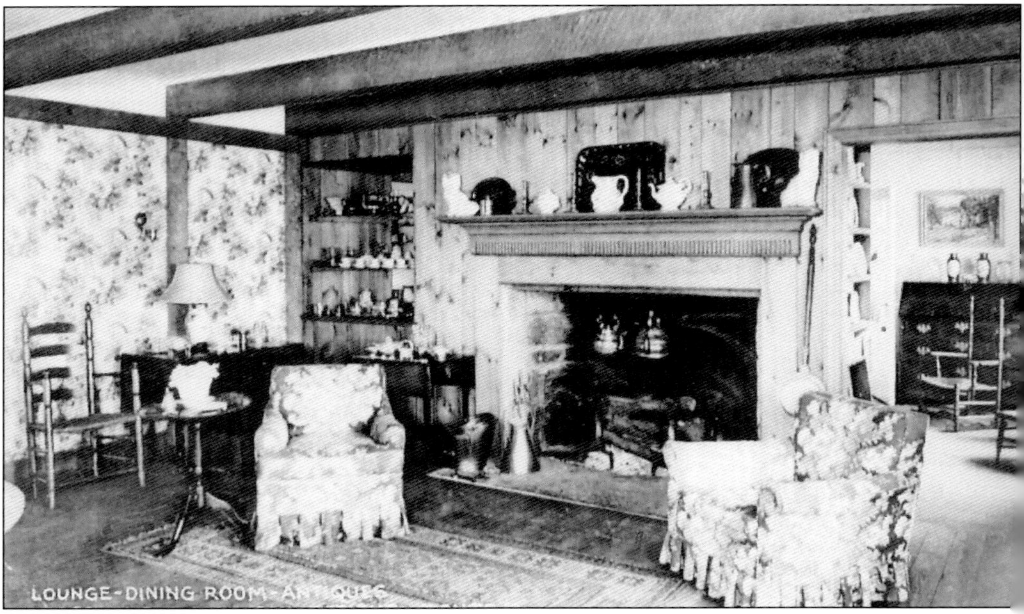

The rooms of the Crossways allowed for the creation of pleasant dining areas. Today, the complement the historic interpretations of the Wilton Heritage Museum.

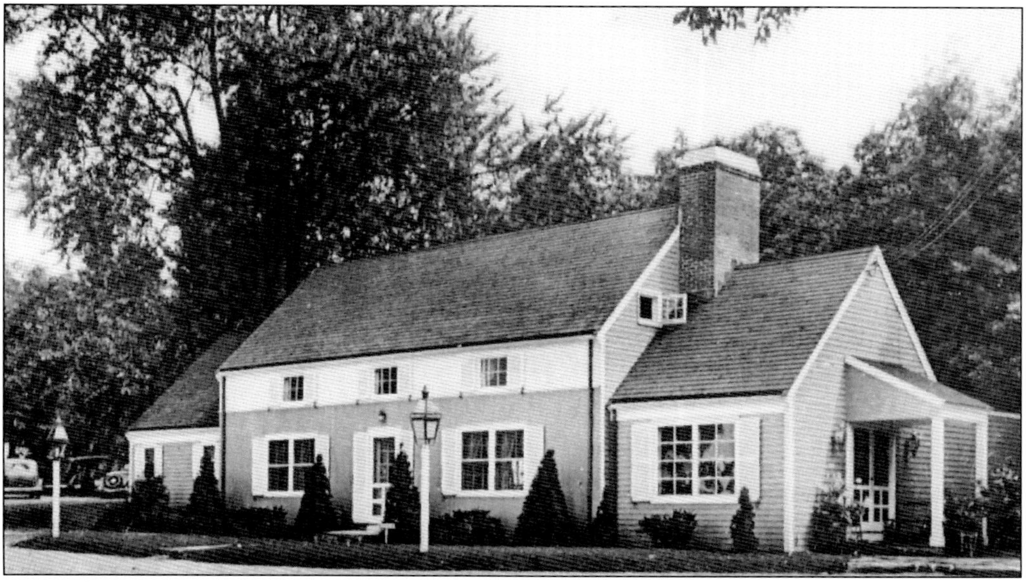

Once the property of Mr. and Mrs. William St. John Comstock, this commercial complex known as the Crossways was first developed by Mr. and Mrs. William Edwards. The couple rearranged the outbuildings and added others. The south end of this structure was for many years the office of Dr. Leonard Maidman, and later that of Dr. Alan Radin.

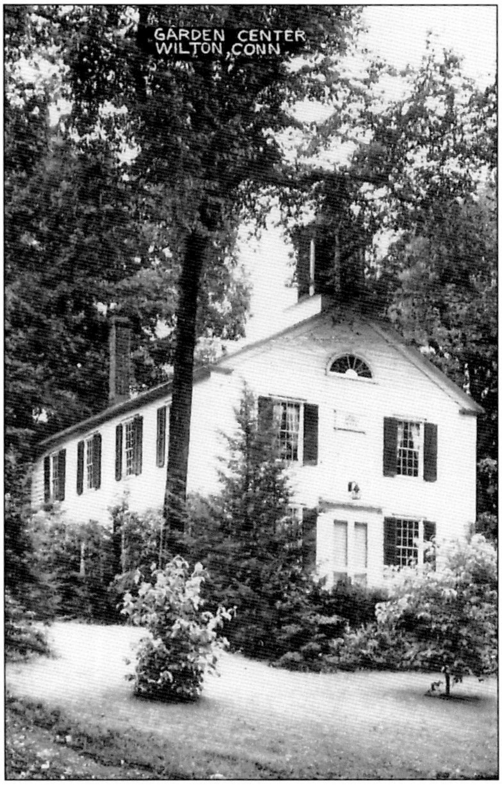

The old town hall was leased to the Wilton Garden Club after 1932 and called The Garden Center. The garden club has renovated the building over the years and continues to use it for their activities.

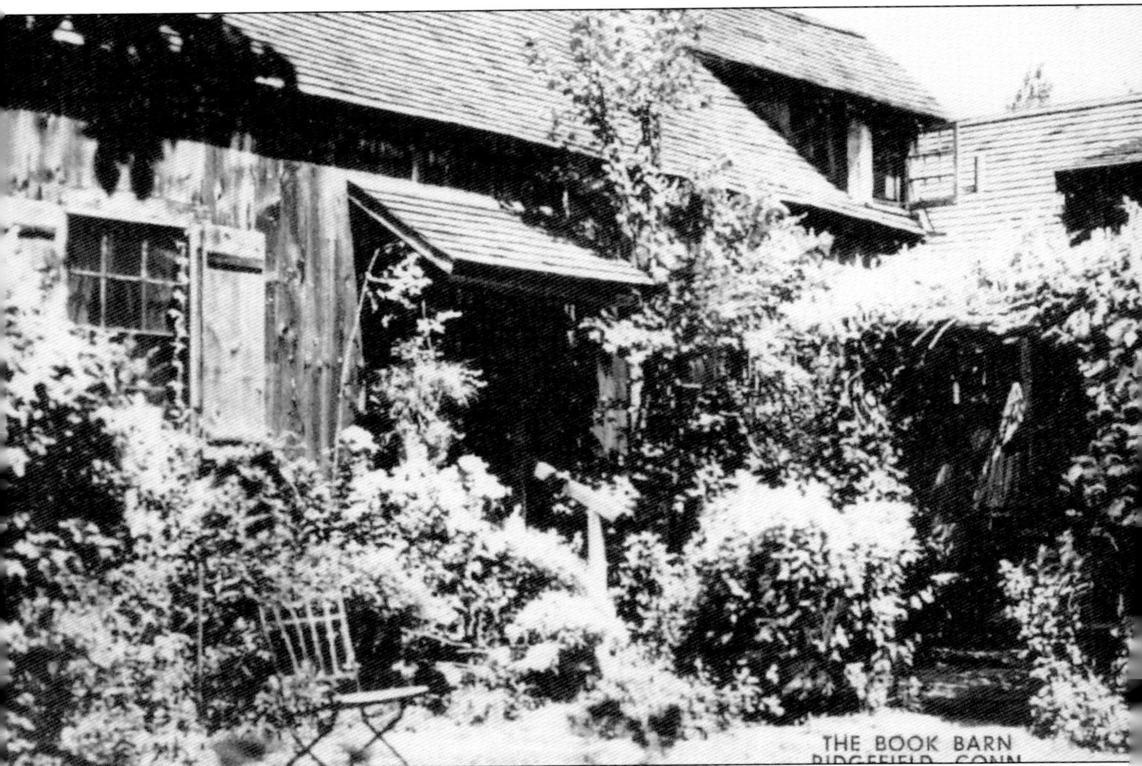

From the 1920s until 1945, this home at 1093 Ridgefield Road was run as a book barn and tearoom by Emily and Fred Gregor, who also lived there. The property straddled the Wilton-

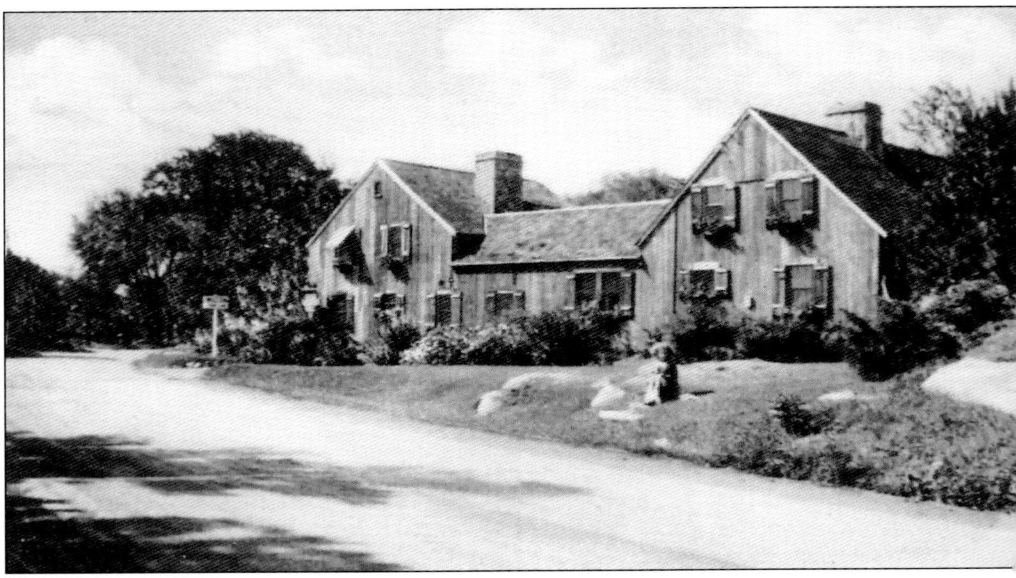

The barn was originally part of the Scott farm across the road.

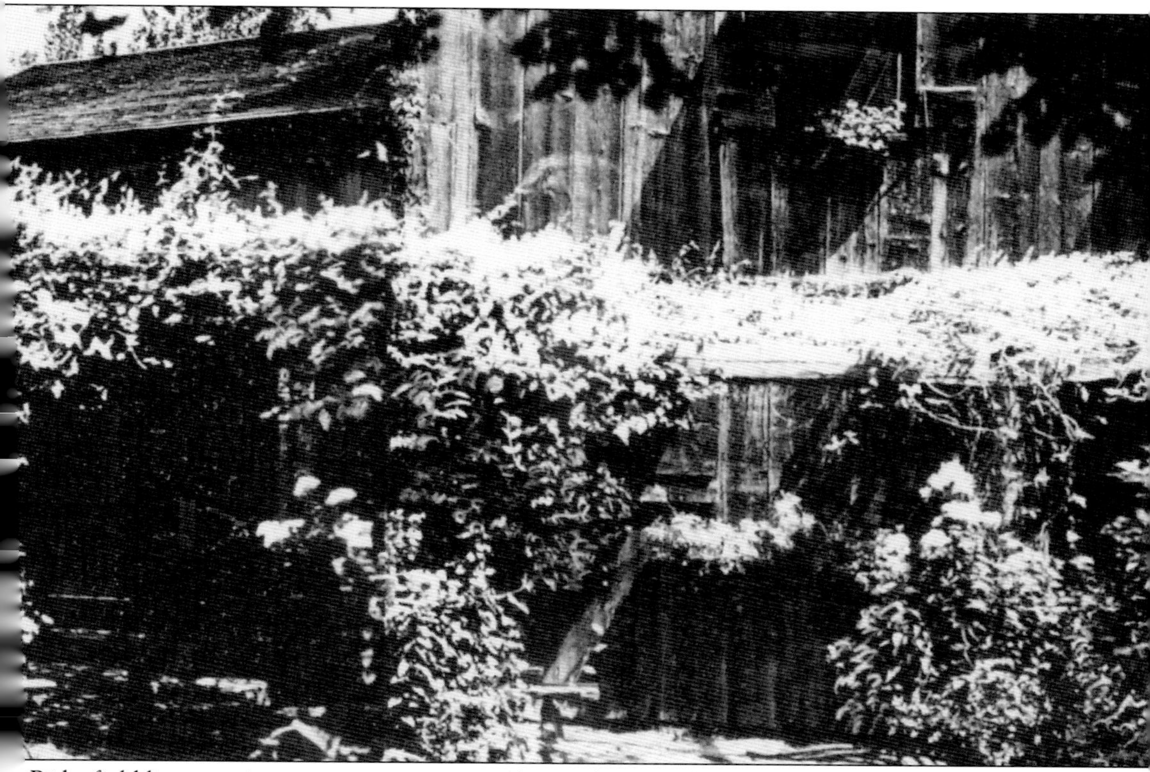

Ridgefield line, causing some inconvenience for residents, such as paying two property tax bills. Among the residents who have stayed there are artists Doris and Sperry Andrews.

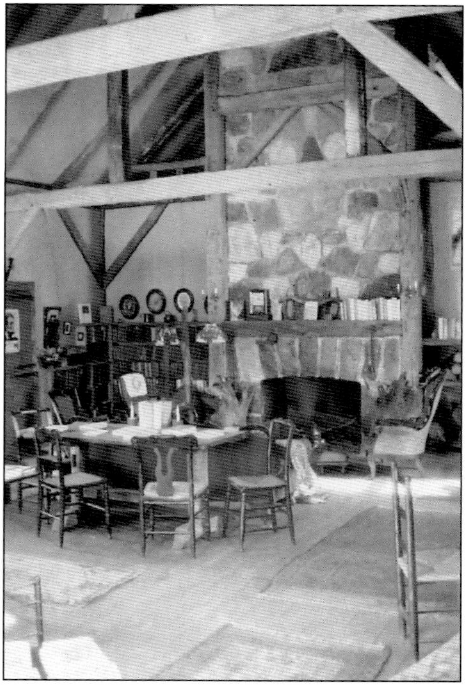

'he interior view shows a pleasant ɔot to sip and browse.

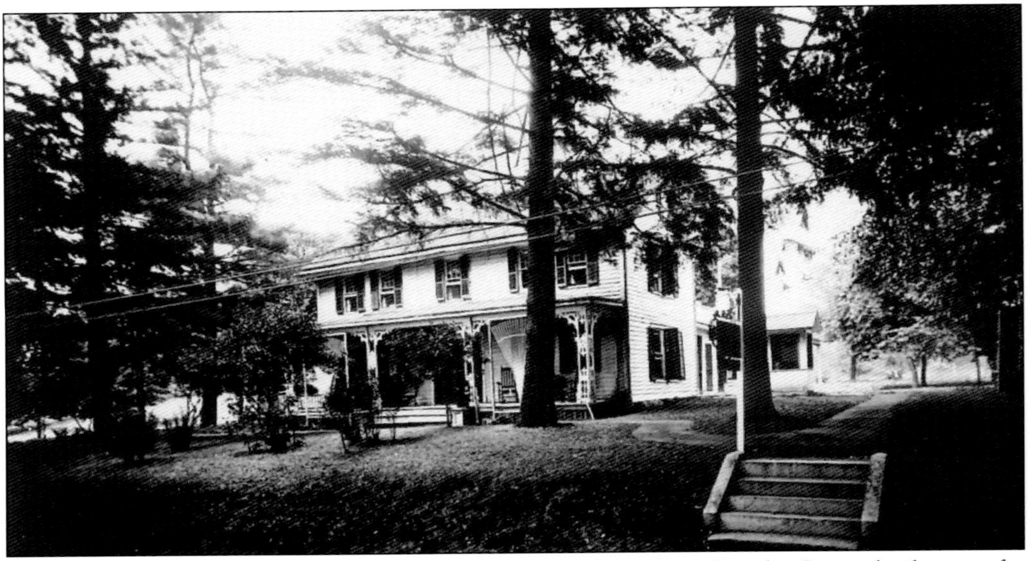

This house is located on the corner of Deerfield and Danbury Roads. Once the home of a Wilton character, Miss Sarah Davenport, it was run as an antique shop and as the Green Lantern Tea House. It has been left to the Wilton Historical Society by Dana Blackmar to be used as a museum.

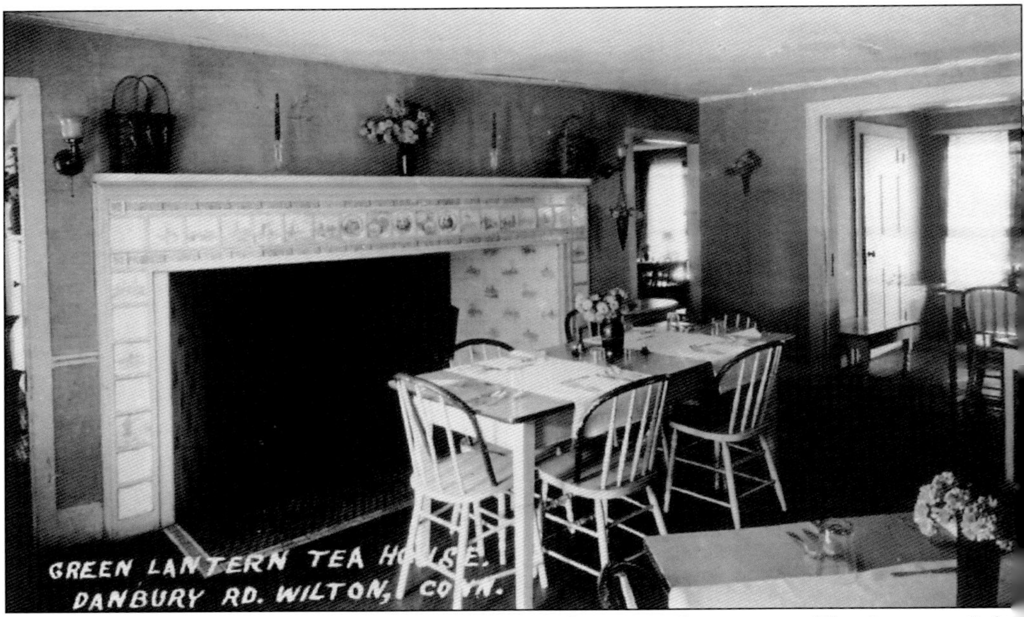

The interior of the Green Lantern Tea House is shown in this picture. The history of th establishment and the particulars surrounding its proprietor and dates are not known.

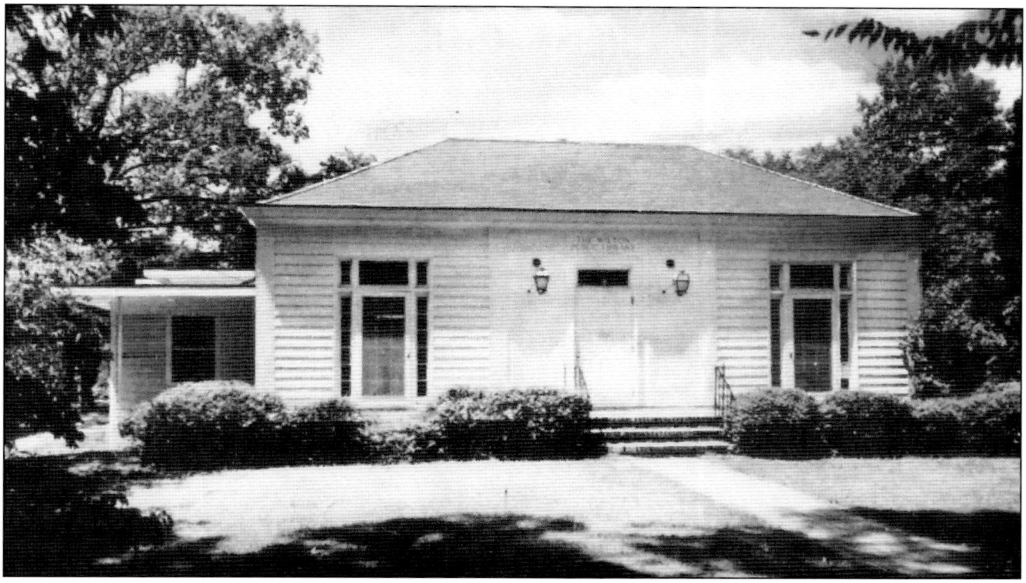

An informal library was organized first at George Taylor's house and then at the studio of H.G. Thomson in 1917. A library building was constructed in 1918. Ethel Hart was librarian for many years, and a Wilton historical society held meetings and kept artifacts in the basement.

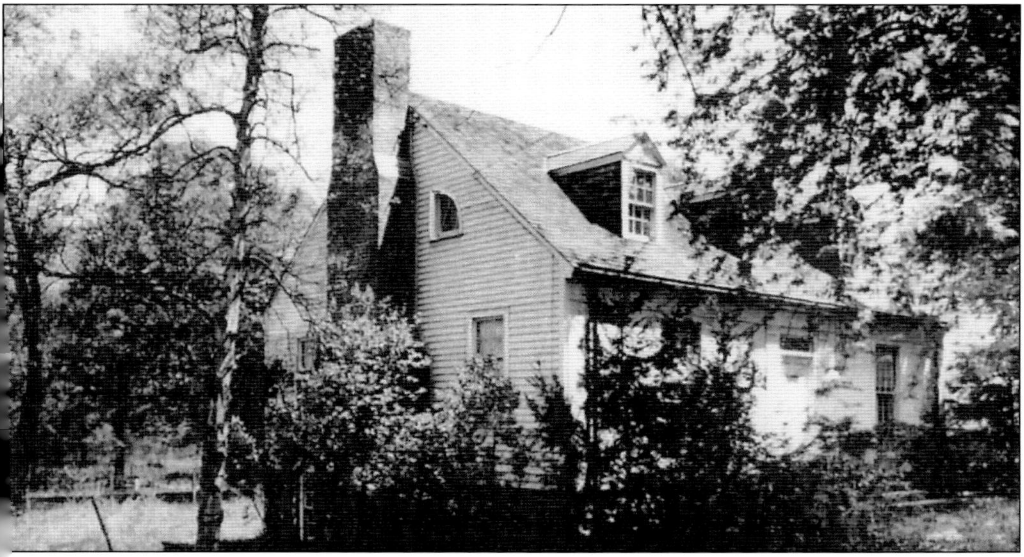

The American Legion Building was built by the Legion members, who were for the most part mployed by Meyer Brothers Construction, a large employer in the early 1900s.

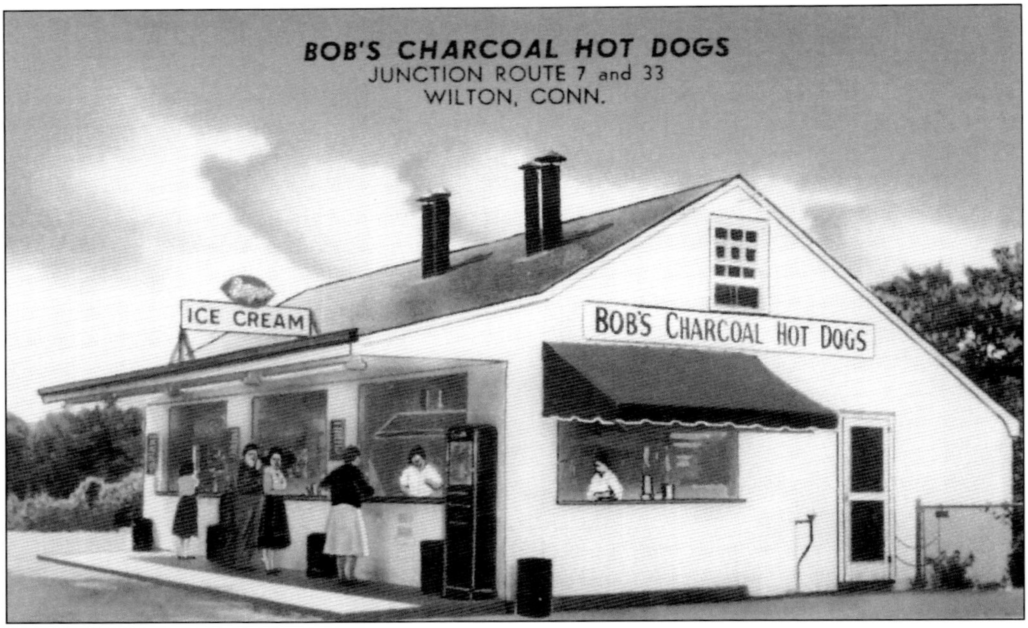

Robert "Bob" Carvutto was the volunteer fire chief, an entrepreneur, and everybody's friend. Involved in an early oil company and in real estate, he established Bob's Charcoal Grill, which became an after-school stopping place for students as well as a friendly place for adults. A delicatessen and gas station are now located at the site.

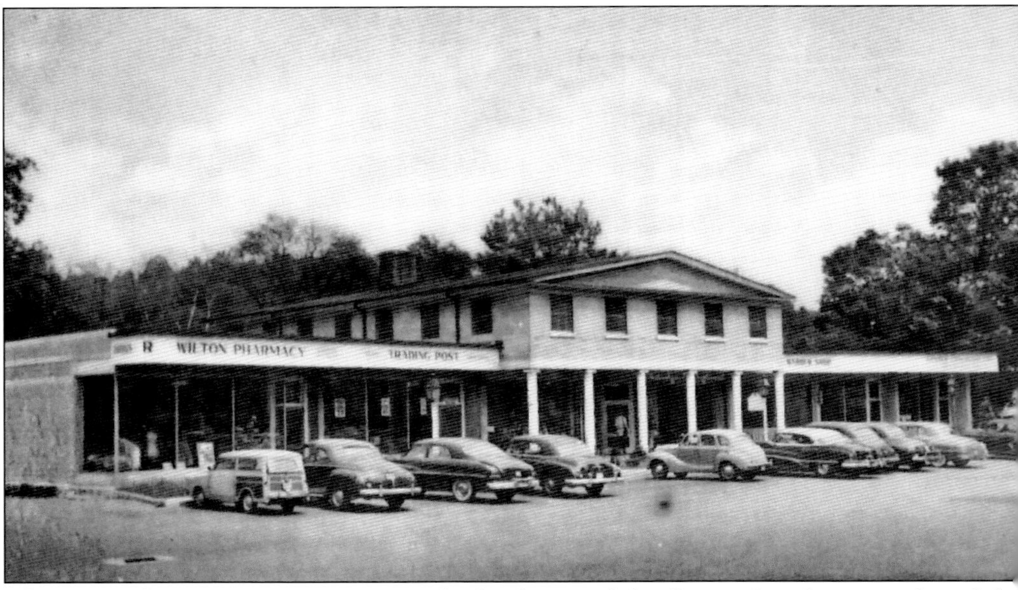

Ed Stivers's drugstore, a grocery store, a barbershop, and the Center Luncheonette shared th early Barringer Building. George Taylor's home is visible just to the south in the picture.

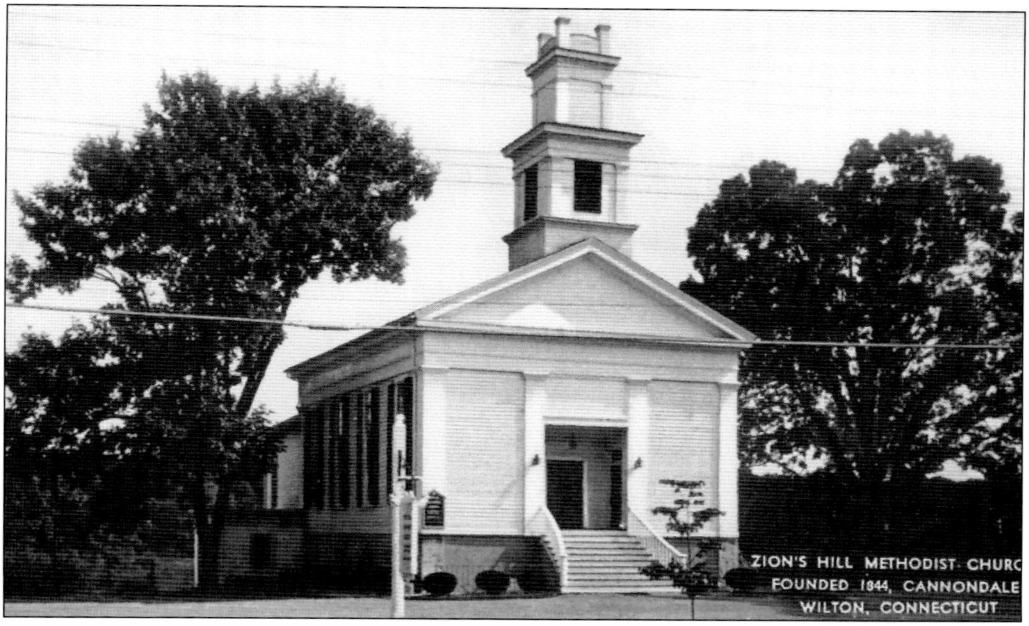

The Zion Hill Methodist Church has maintained an active fellowship since 1844. It has added a meeting hall and shares a Strawberry Festival and nursery school with the community.

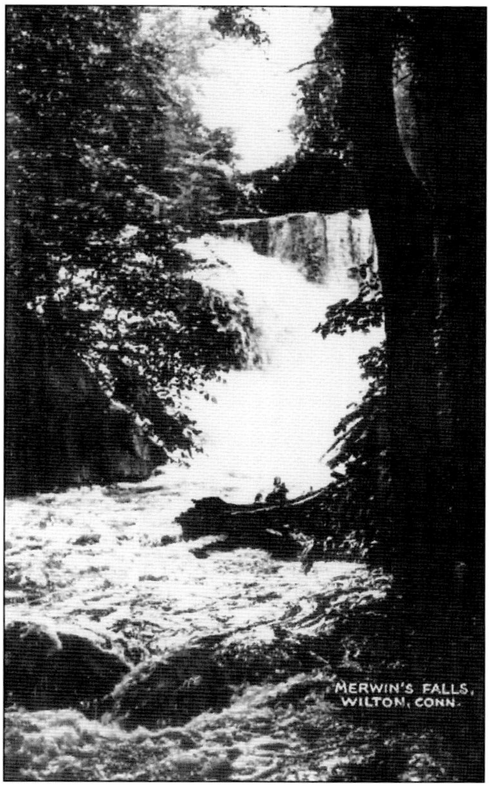

The old mill stream, seen in this Edward Wells card, continues to flow heavily over the old dam in a time of high water to the enjoyment of hikers.

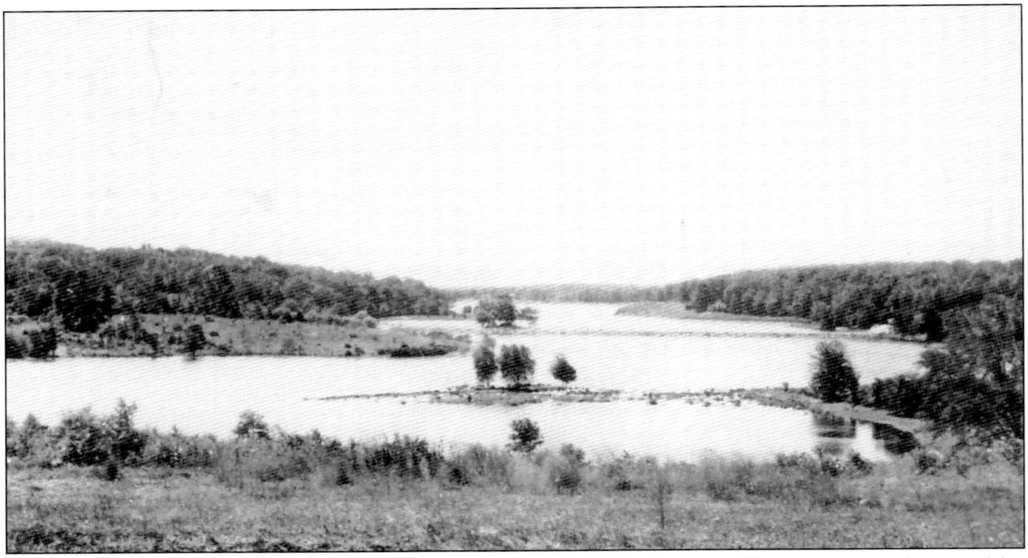

Several postcard companies have pictured the Norwalk Reservoir. The image on this card by Edward Wells was taken from Drum Hill.

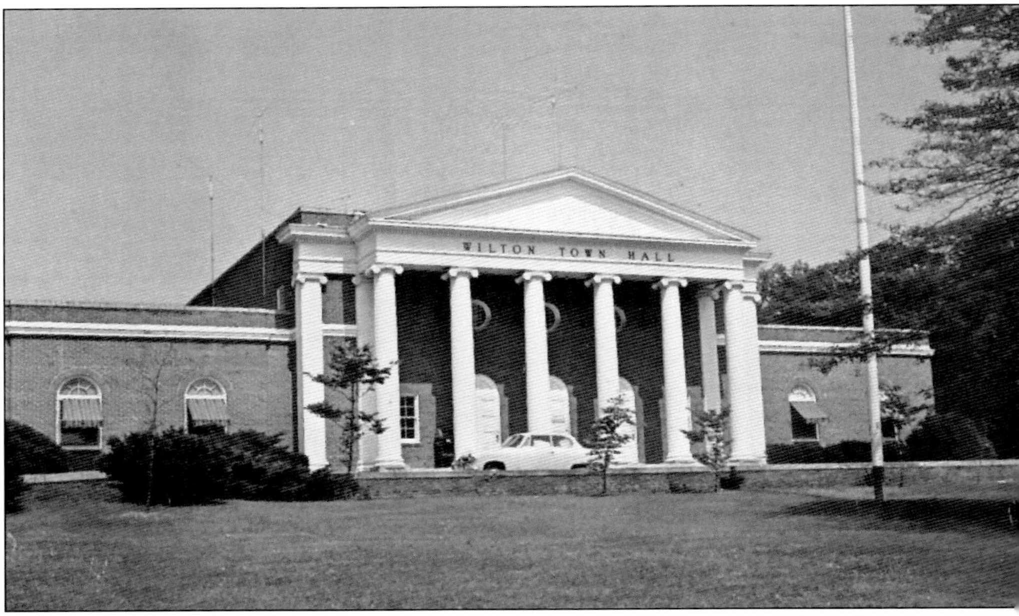

Wilton's town hall, its cornerstone laid in 1930, included an auditorium where dances, minstre shows, school plays, and political meetings were held. It once saw firemen's carnivals wher now it sees a modern firehouse, police station, and office annex.

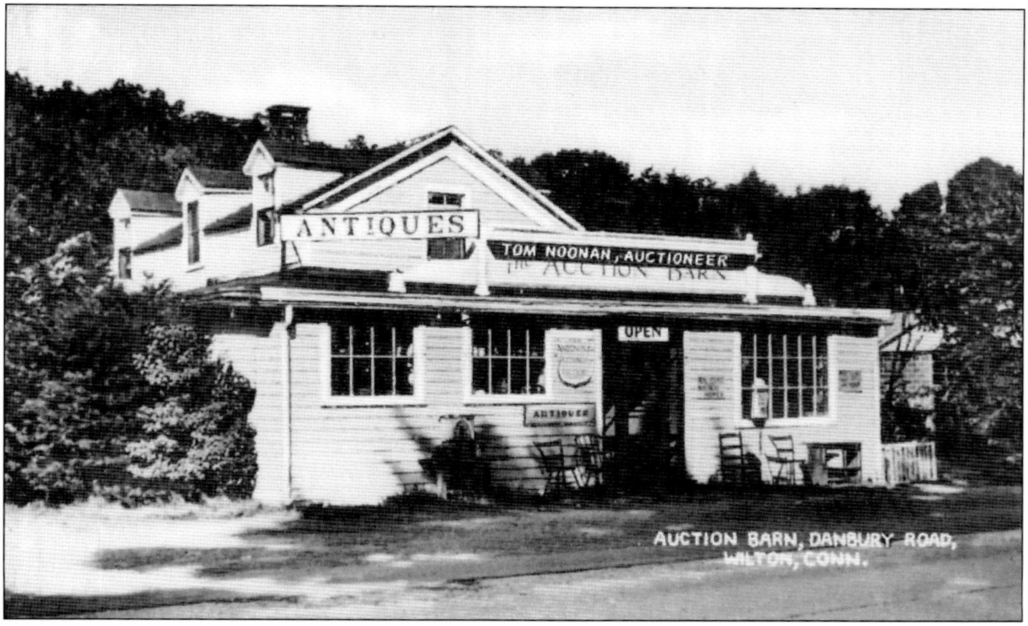

Tom and Trudy Noonan ran an antique shop opposite Wolfpit Road from the 1940s to the 1970s in the building that had once housed the office of Wilton's first undertaker, Mr. James Taylor. A copy of his record book is in the New Canaan Historical Society library, thanks to Mary L. Sturges. As a small grocery store run by the Spicers and then the McNamaras, the building welcomed neighborhood children on their skates from Meyers' Pond for warmth and penny candy.

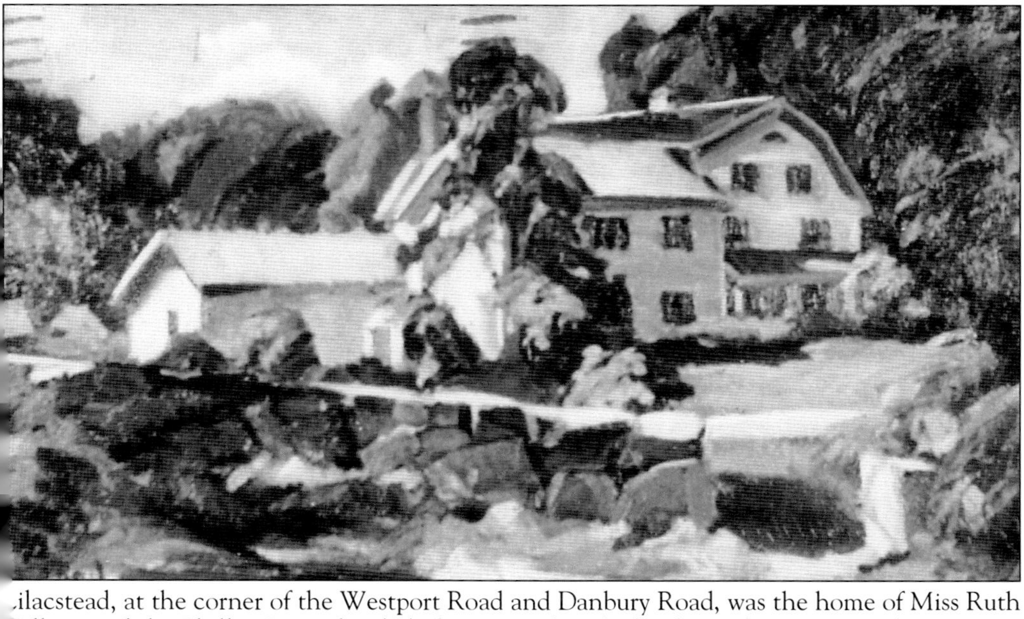

.ilacstead, at the corner of the Westport Road and Danbury Road, was the home of Miss Ruth :ellogg and the Phillip Gregg family before it was bought by the Wilton Historical Society. It s now called Lambert House.

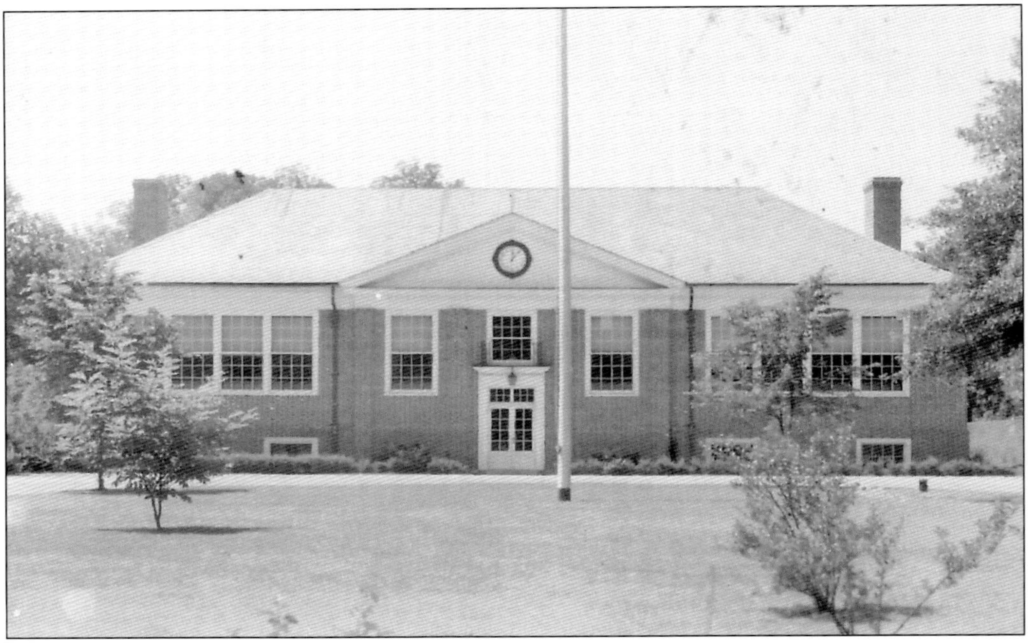

About 1929, the four-room Center School was built, bringing together the pupils from Wilton's one-room district schools. The building was later enlarged and has been remodeled into a commercial center.

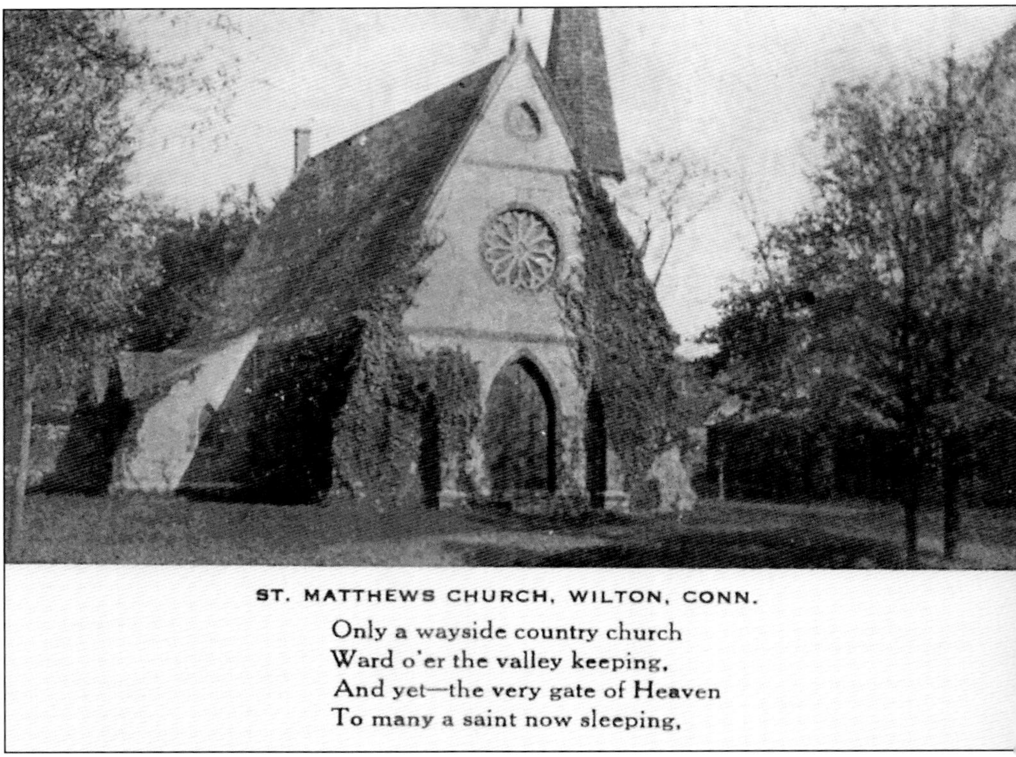

This view of the stone church is accompanied by a poem composed by Eva Ogden Lambert.

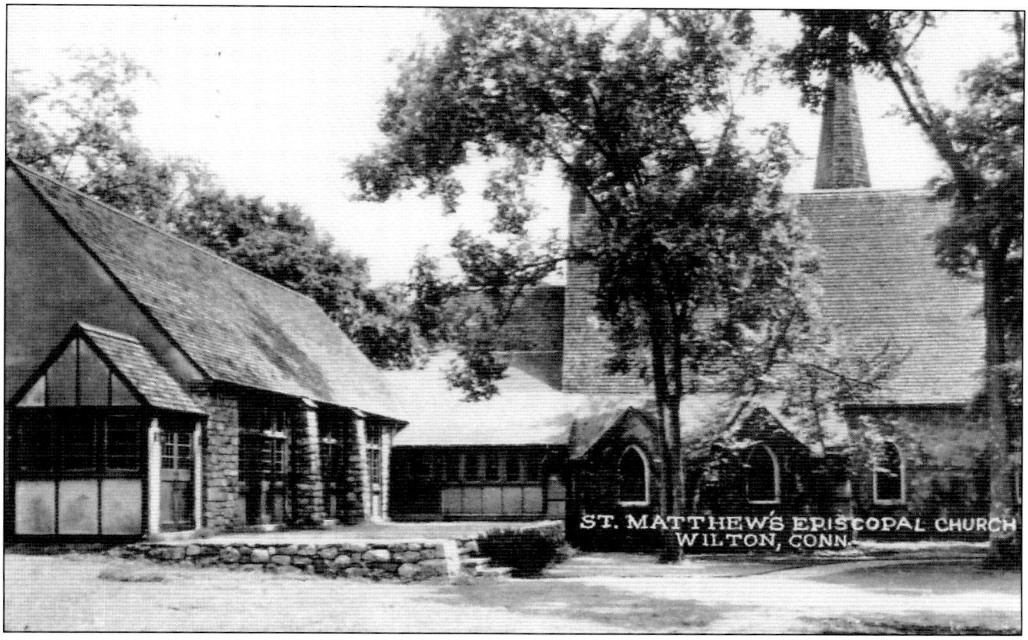

A "Canterbury Market" was held at the Episcopal church for many years, with games, food, and a costumed monk riding on a donkey. With the growth of the parish, a large hall, offices, and Sunday school space were added.

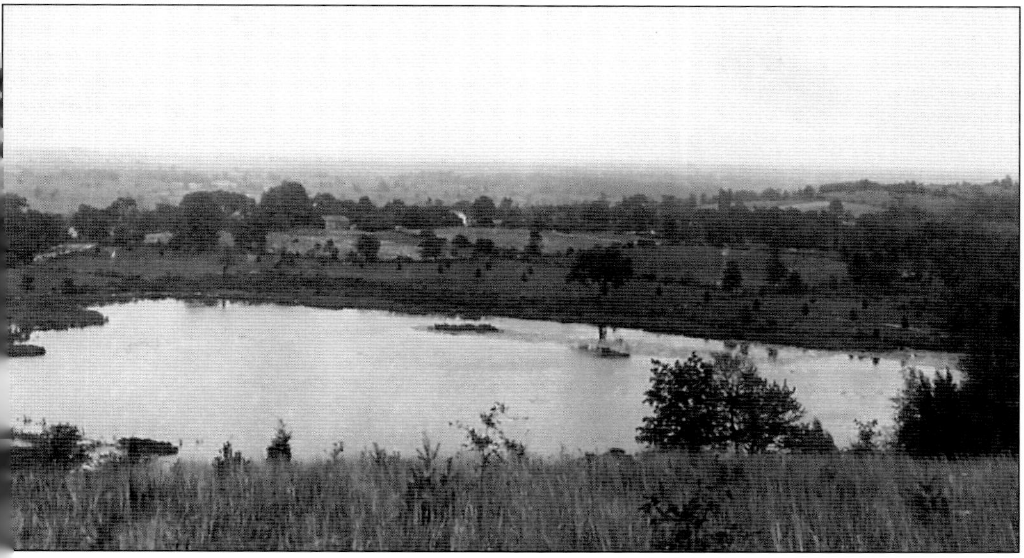

'his property was owned first by the Keeler family and then later by a Mr. Kent. A geodesic ıarker on Bald Hill indicates that the property encompasses one of the highest points in airfield County.

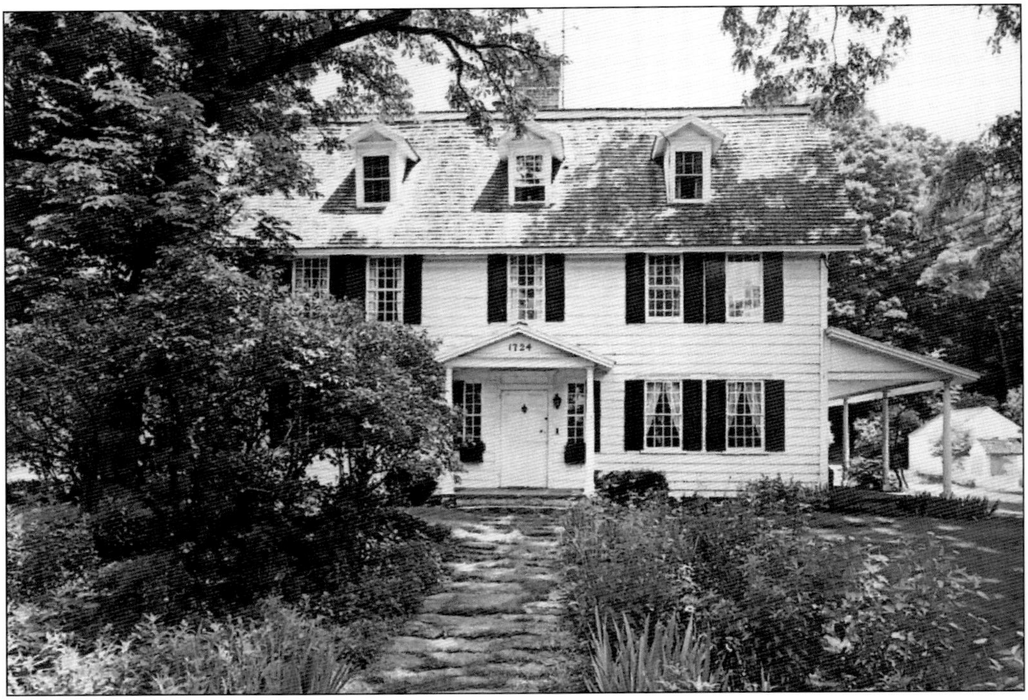

Lambert House has become the focal point in a complex of several older Wilton buildings that have been moved to this property.

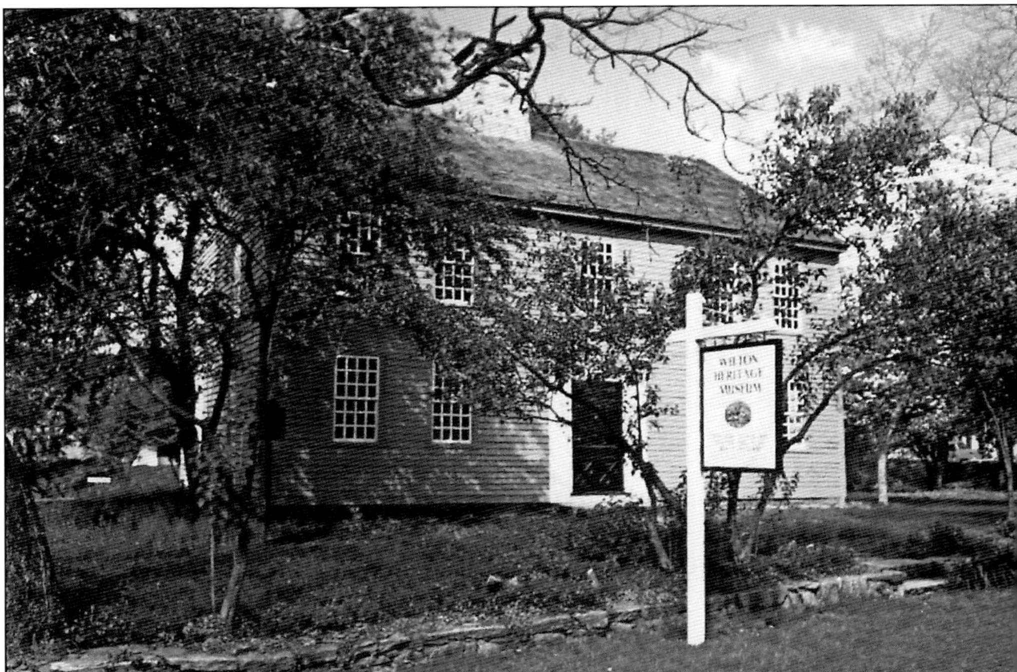

This is another historical building whose preservation exemplifies the aim of the Wilton Historical Society to maintain the best of Wilton's past.

Five

Wilton Joins the World

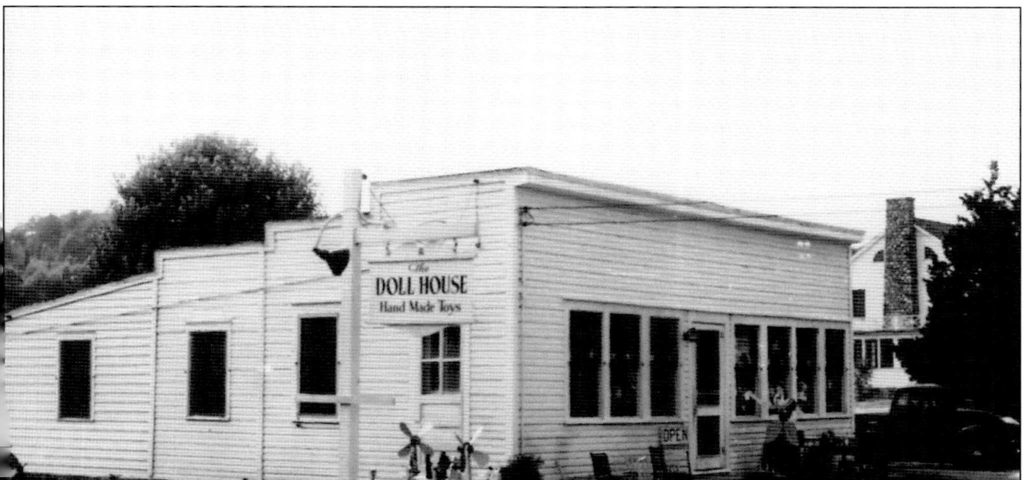

This small building has had several uses. The Lawrence family lived in it while constructing the house shown to the north. It was also the antique shop of Mr. and Mrs. Thomas Fitzsimmons. The 1950 issue of the town yearbook by the League of Women Voters lists it as a gift shop run by Mrs. Sunderland.

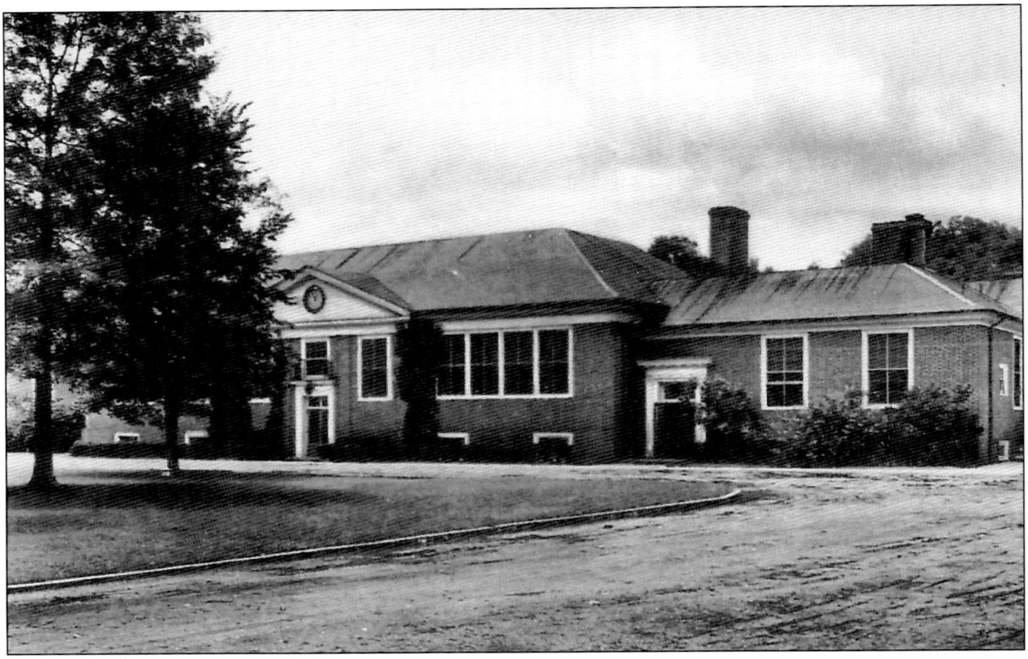

An addition to the four-room Center School was constructed, creating a north wing with an office, an auditorium, and a nurses' room. The school housed grades one through eight.

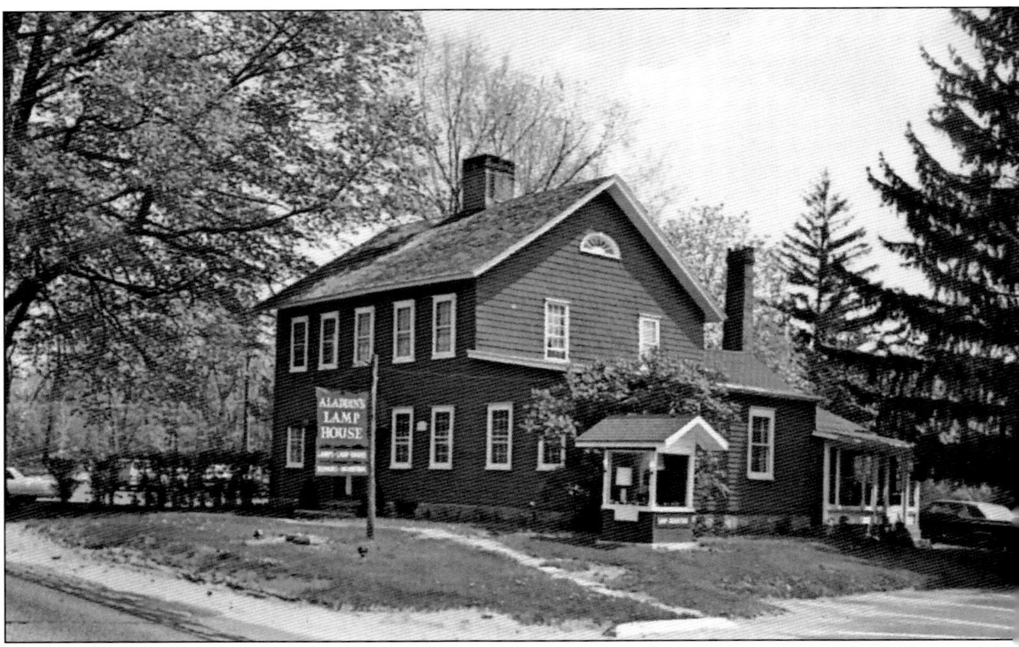

Many old homes have succumbed to commercialism, and then the wrecking ball. One of th first to go in the South Wilton area was Madison Cooper's Lamp House at 26 Danbury Road.

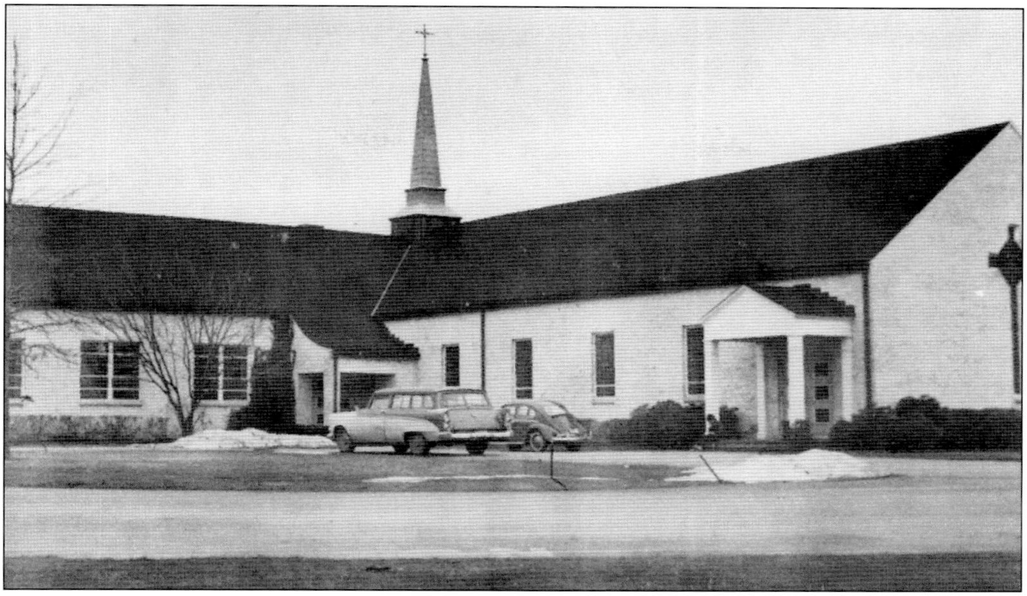

Our Lady of Fatima Church was built on the former property of the Ogden family. Previously, the closest Catholic churches were in Norwalk, Georgetown, or Ridgefield.

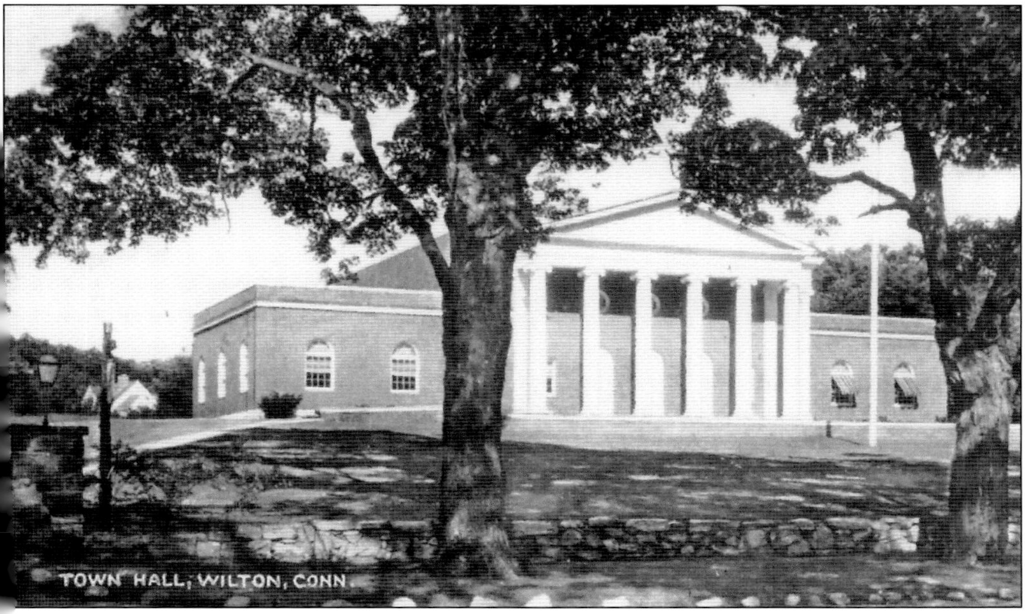

Iere is another view of the town hall. This image was produced by the Edward Wells Company.

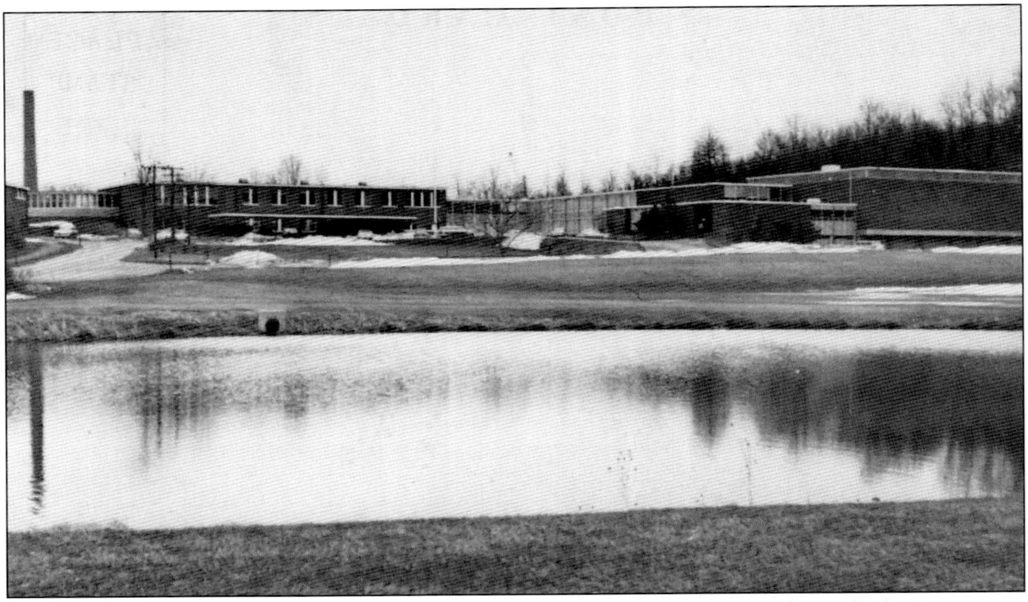

This school was renamed Cider Mill School in memory of a historic cider mill that was once located roughly on this site. At the time the photograph was taken, the building was known as Wilton Junior High School.

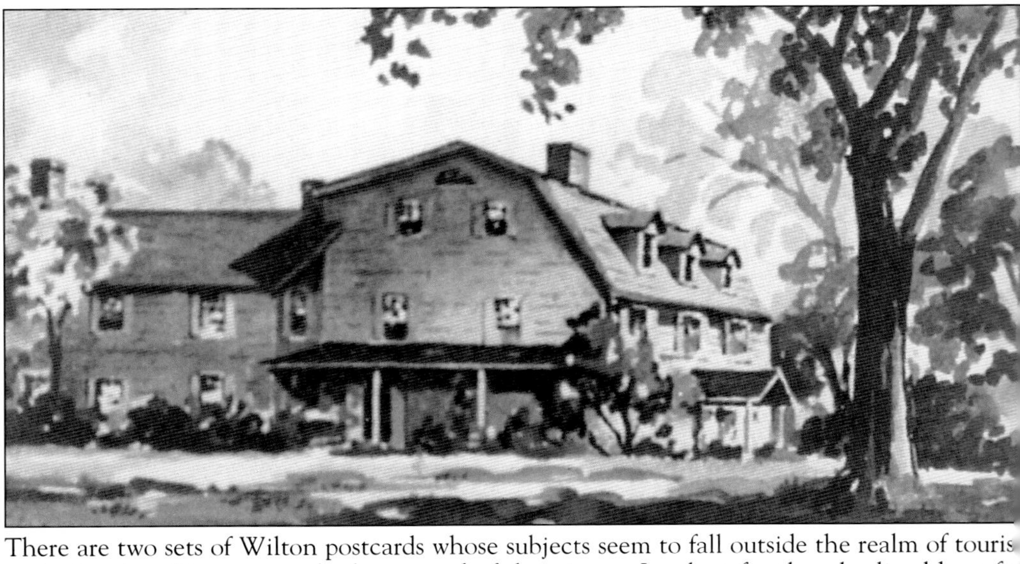

There are two sets of Wilton postcards whose subjects seem to fall outside the realm of touris cards. Lambert Tavern was the homestead of the pioneer Lambert family, who lived here fo several generations.

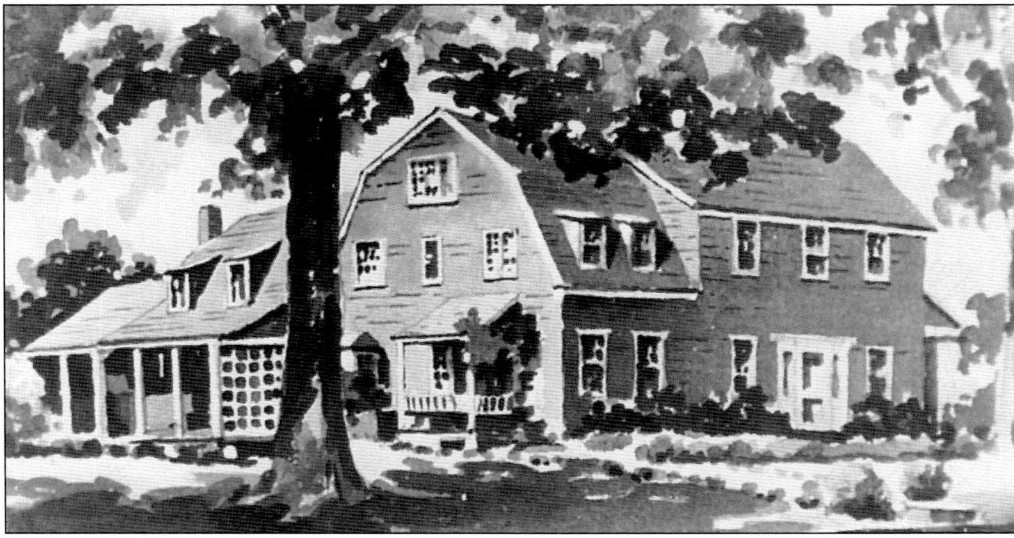

The Matthew Gregory House, still lived in by the Gregory family, overlooks the reservoir on Belden Hill Road.

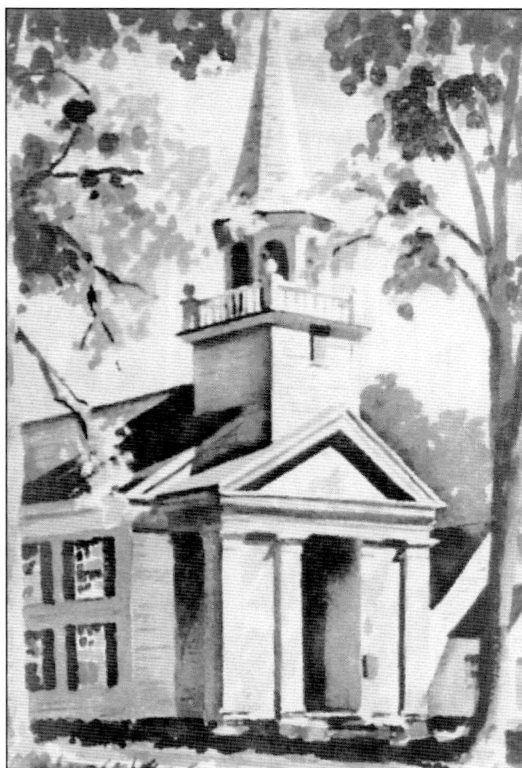

The Wilton Meeting House (Congregational), so titled in this set, once had a small parish hall next door.

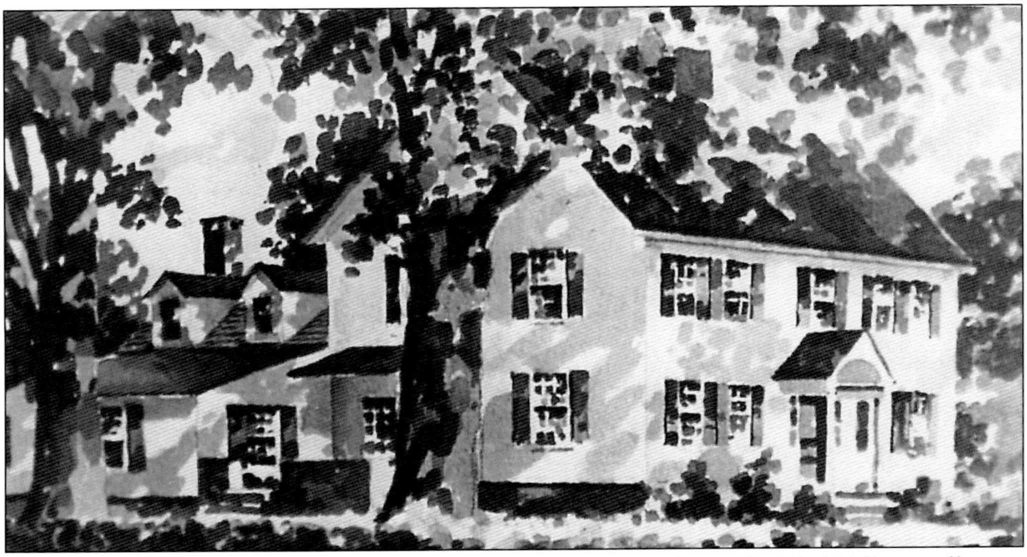

The Alexander Resseguie house stands on the Ridgefield Road near the Nod Hill turnoff.

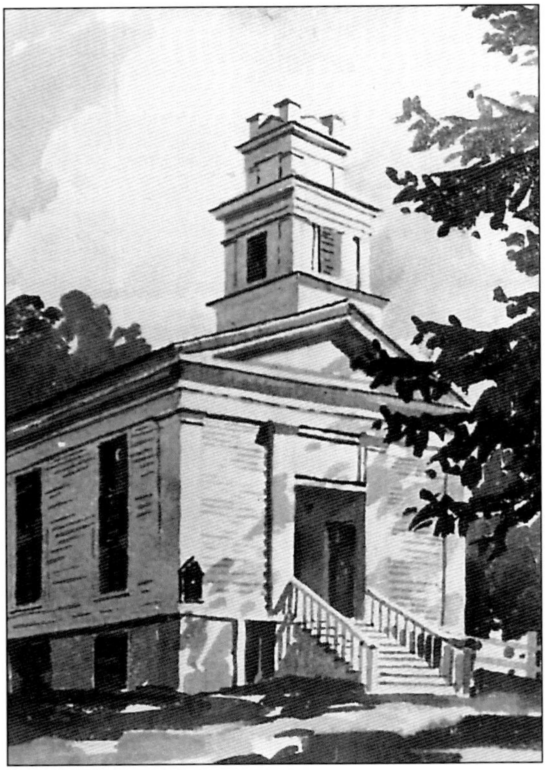

The Zion Hill Church, here flanked by its cemetery, is a classic style Methodist church structure.

The Wilton Academy and Town Hall building was the site of the well-known school started by Hawley Olmstead and continued by his son, Edward.

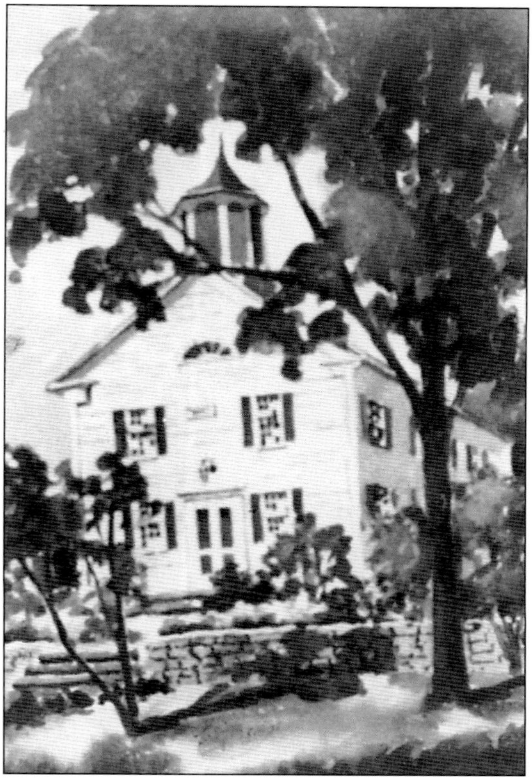

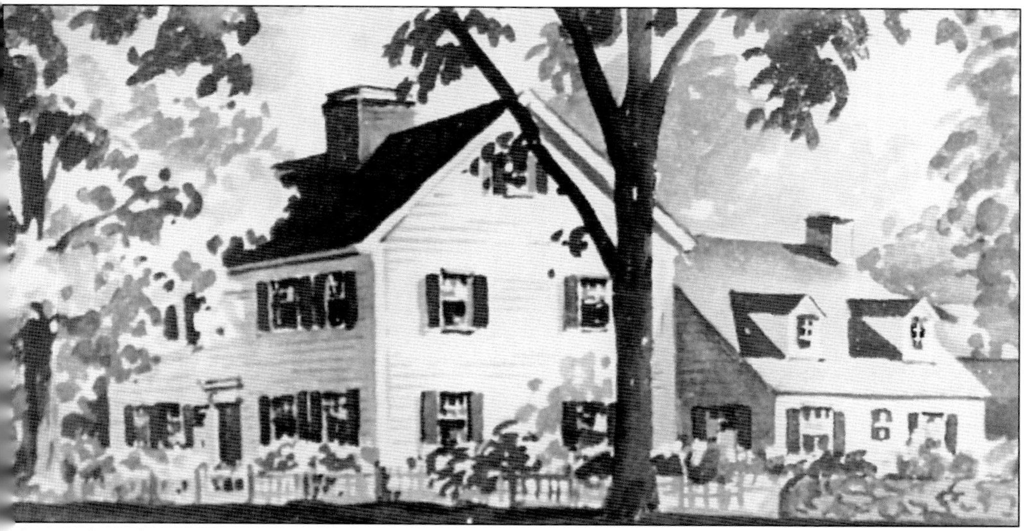

lexander Sloane was an early owner of this property, probably living in the small original ection at the rear.

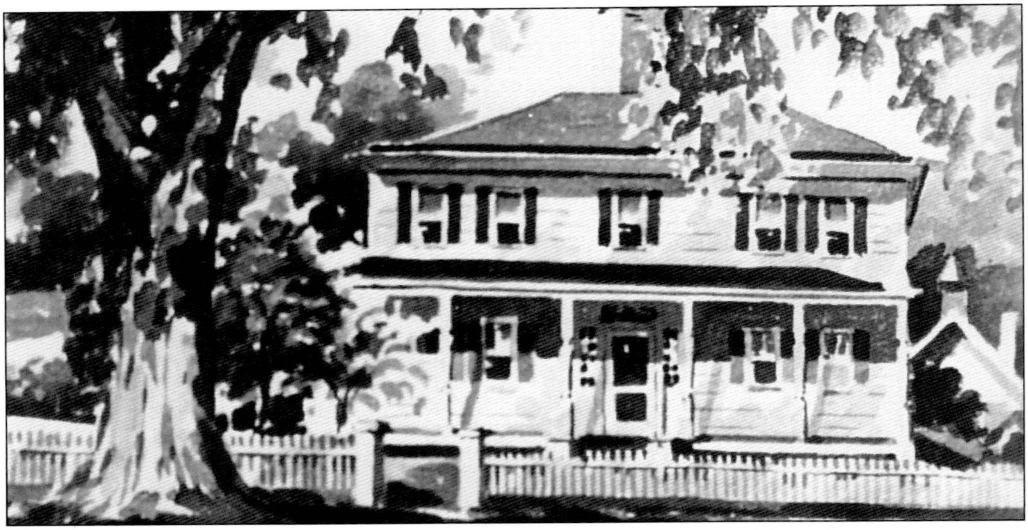

Marvin Tavern, a place with Revolutionary origins, was documented by a diary entry written by a passing soldier.

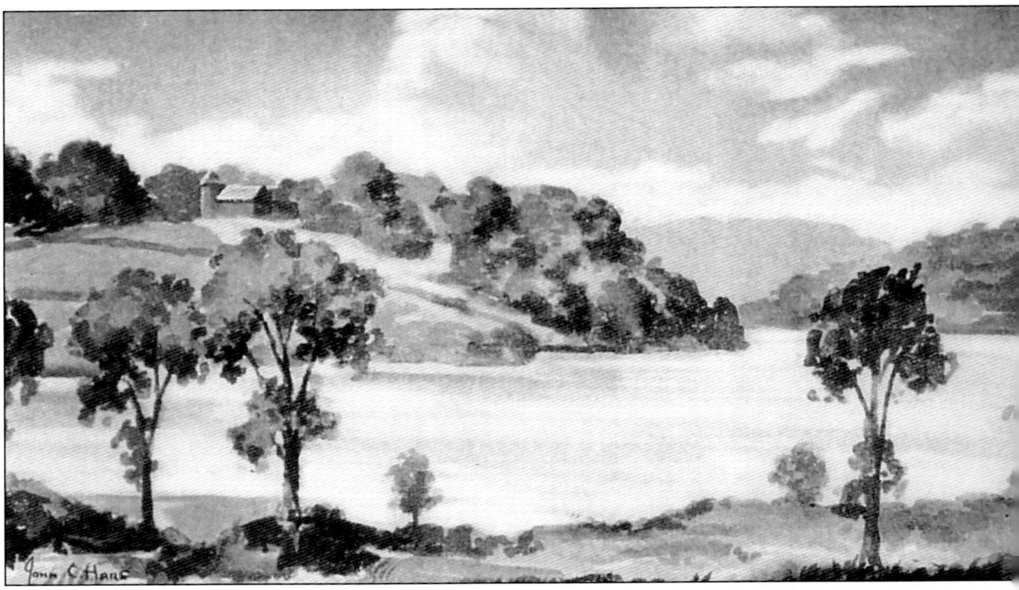

The next set of images shows scenes signed by John C. Hare. Hare must have spent some tim in Wilton, as the views cover the years 1933–36. The view from Nod Hill includes the man made lake known variously as Pope's or Street's Pond.

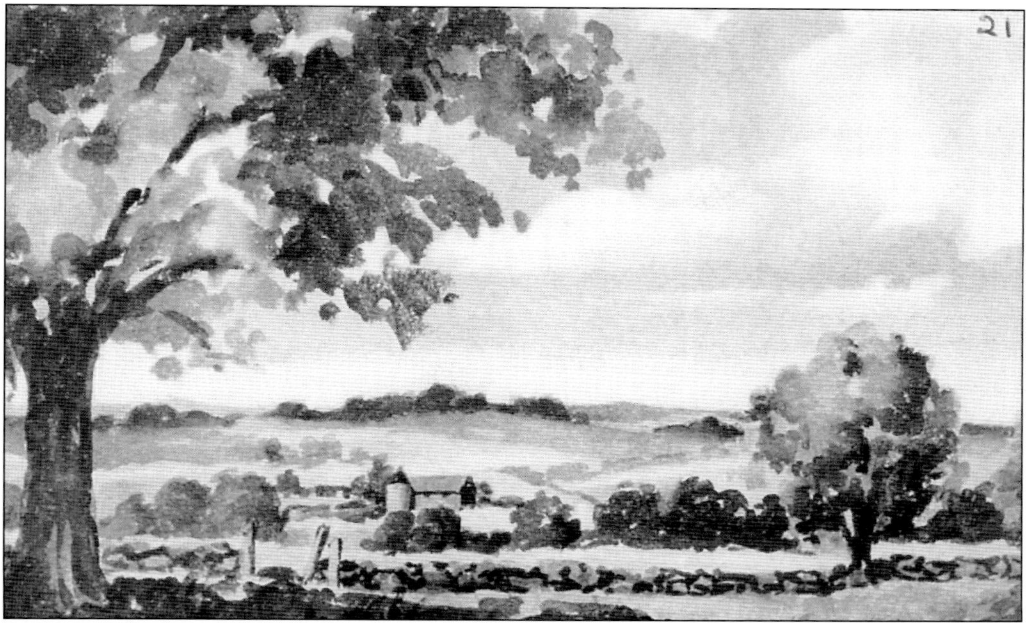

Turner's Ridge looks over the area where Dr. Edward Turner planned to build his sanitarium for women who had become alcoholics (the facility was planned before the possibility of female alcoholism was accepted). Turner was not to succeed in Wilton, but did become the head of a sanitarium in New York State.

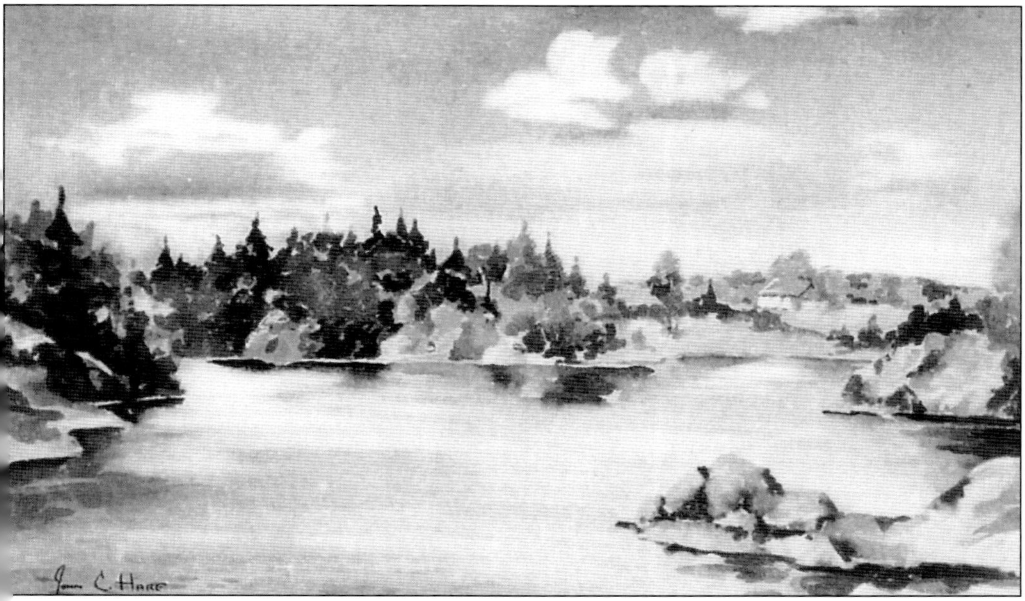

The upper reservoir, still part of the Norwalk water supply system, was the site of one of the Old Leatherman's stopovers, a place located under a ledge, during the nomad's regular rounds in the New York and Connecticut area.

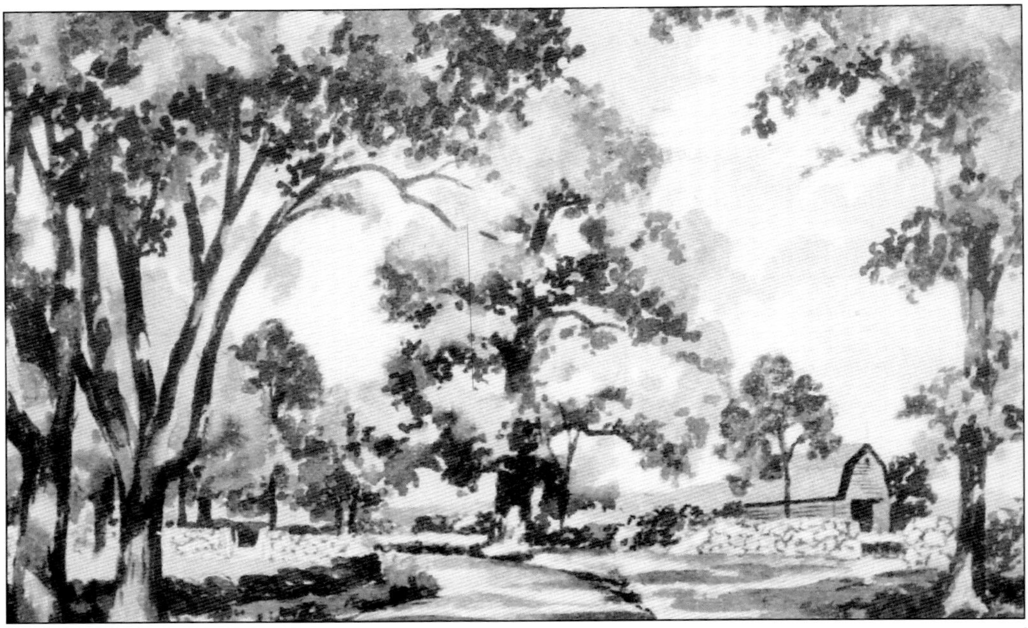

This view of the Ridgefield Road, approximately opposite Drum Hill Road, was probably one of the John Hare set.

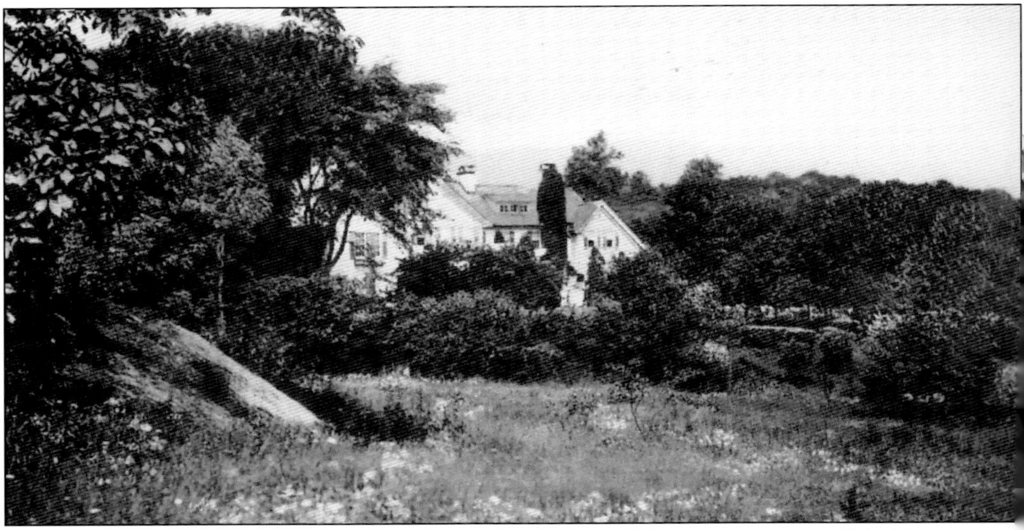

Many large homes were built in the 1930s, when other old homes were remodeled by summe residents. This estate located across the road from Kent Pond was owned by the Moran an then the Eason families.

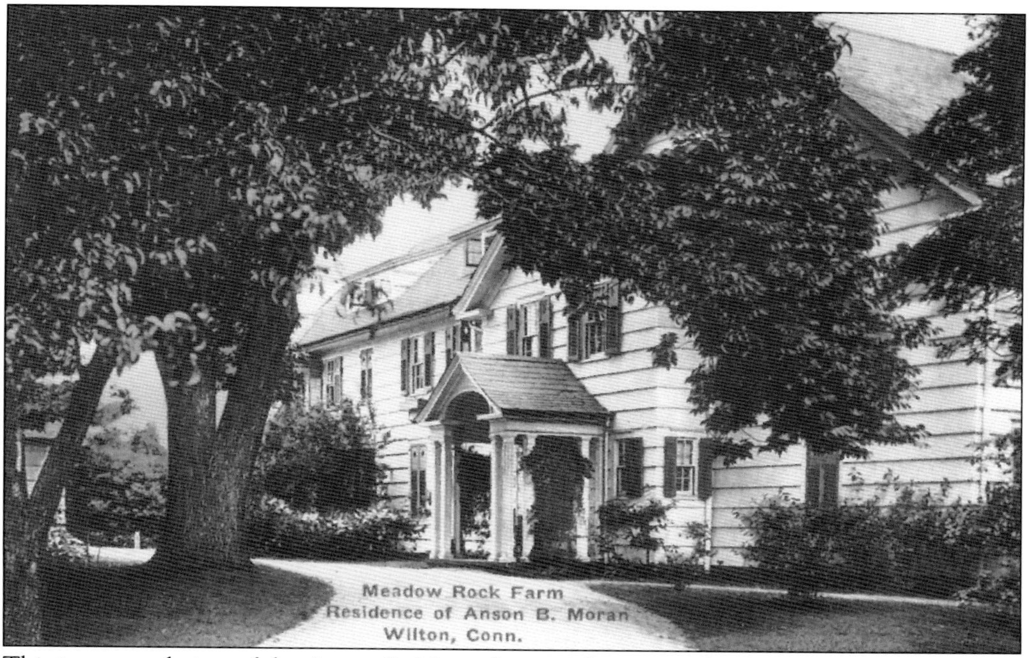

This is a second view of the Anson B. Moran house. Moran is said to have had a nine-hole golf course in his back meadow. The postcards, printed by the Albertype Company, were published by the H.P. Bissell Company in Ridgefield.

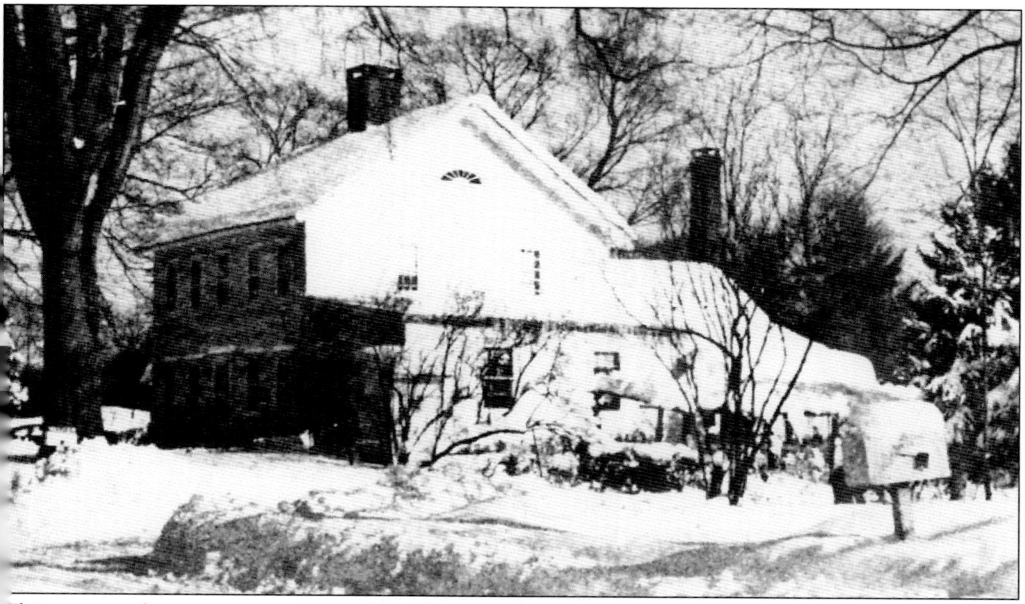

ˈhis postcard was apparently used by the Harold Walker family as a Christmas card in 1948. ˈhe Walker house in South Wilton had previously been (at various points in time) the Cottage ɜrocery, the Belding Antique Shop, Cooper's Lamp House, and the Clog Hut.

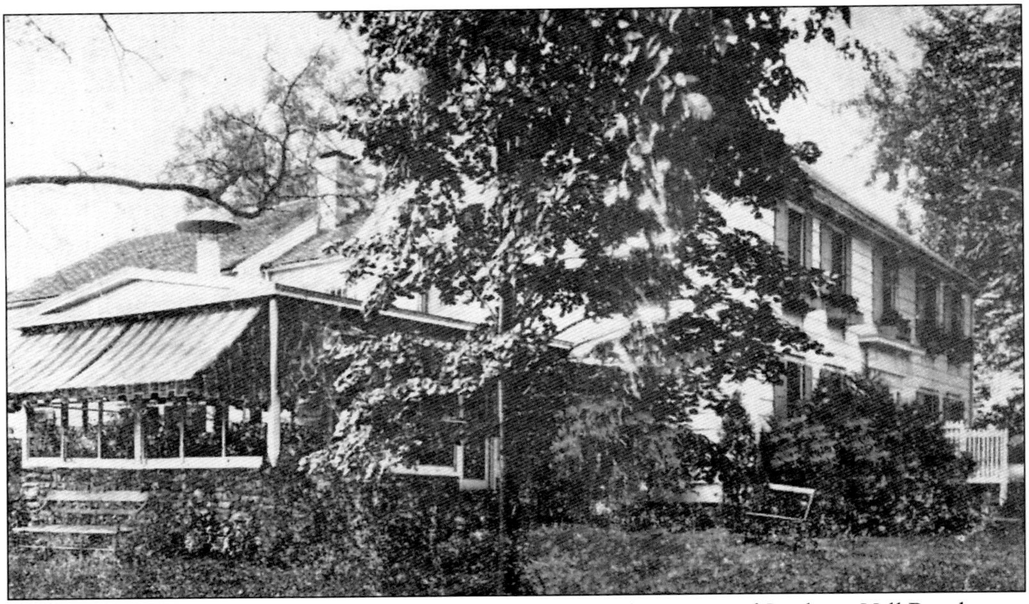

The Split Rock, which is still visible in Cannondale near the corner of Scribner Hill Road, gave the name to the tavern run briefly by Mildred and Reginald Squire. French cuisine was served in an old house that was once part of the farm known as Egypt.

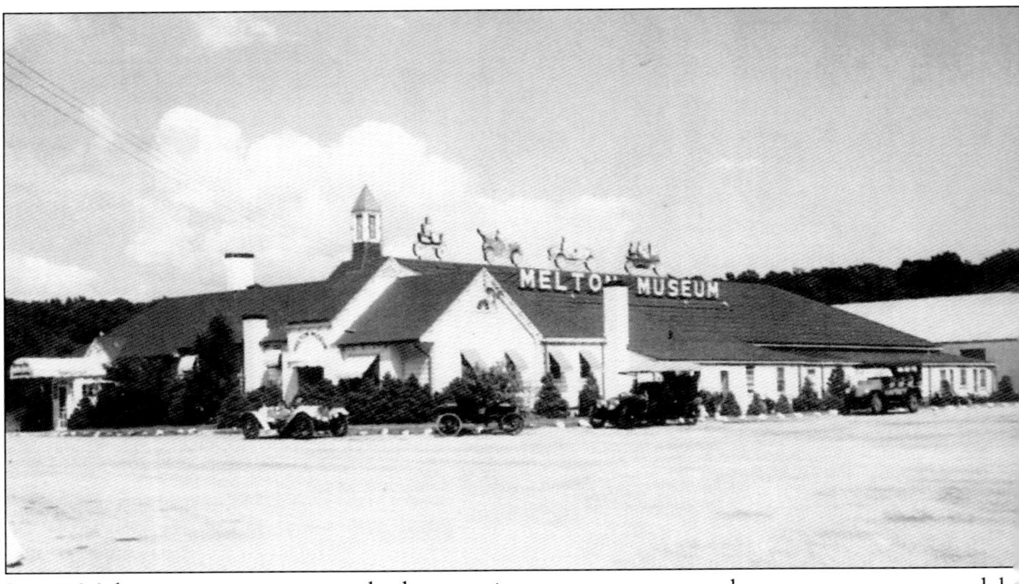

James Melton, an opera singer, had an antique car museum and a restaurant managed b Lawrence Graham. The museum was eventually moved to Florida, and the Caldor Shoppin Center moved in its place.

Six

Old Friends and Neighbors

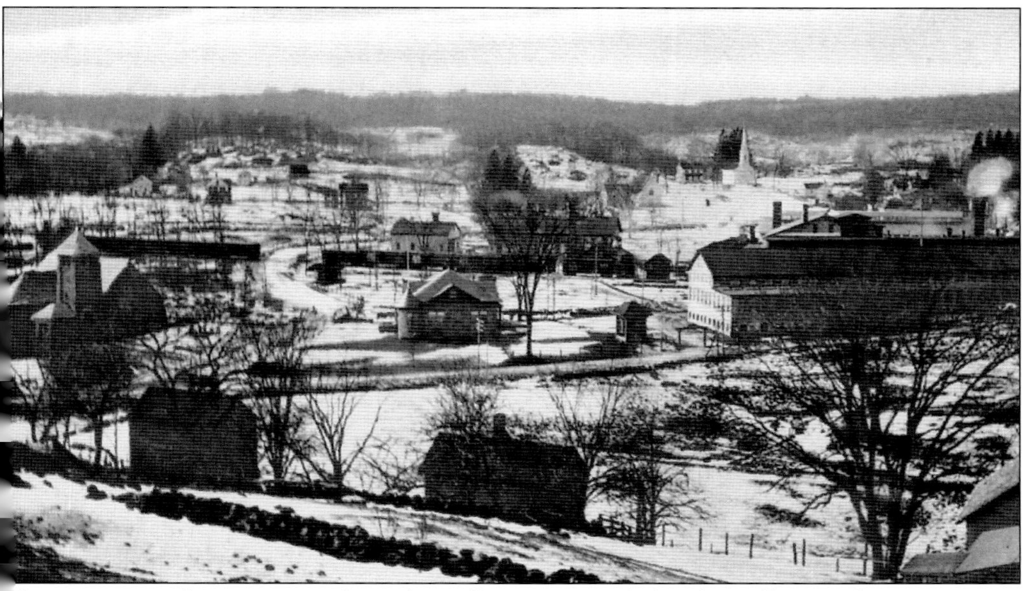

'his overview of Georgetown from the Gilbert Farm includes the Gilbert and Bennett Wire ⁄ill, which for years was the attraction for immigrant laborers and their families.

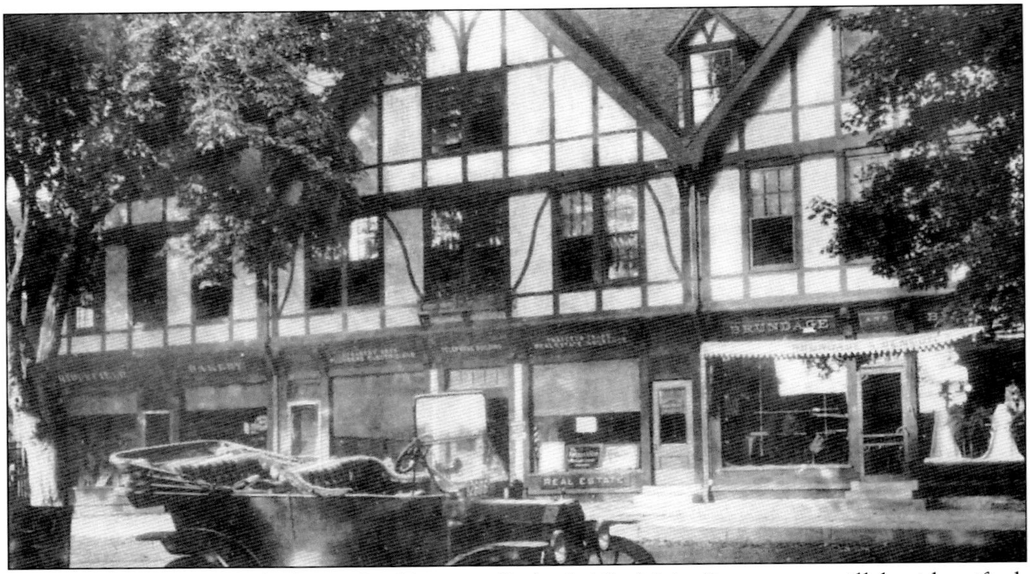

In this picture, the Telephone Building on Ridgefield's Main Street can still be identified, although the automobiles and area shops have changed. This card was published by Morris Berman of New Haven.

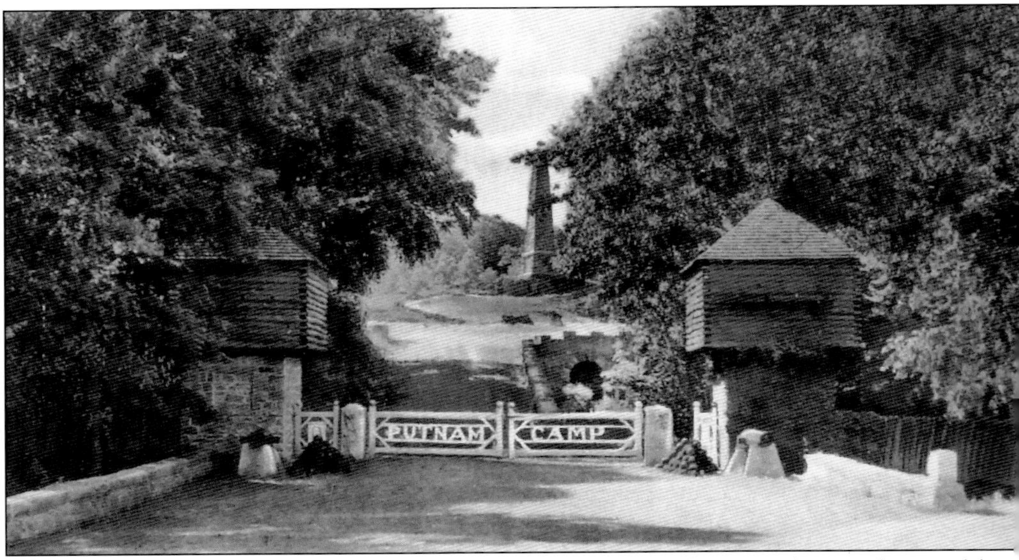

Although Israel Putnam was not a Redding native, this Revolutionary hero is honored by state park in that town. This lithochrome postcard shows the gates, monument, and th block houses.

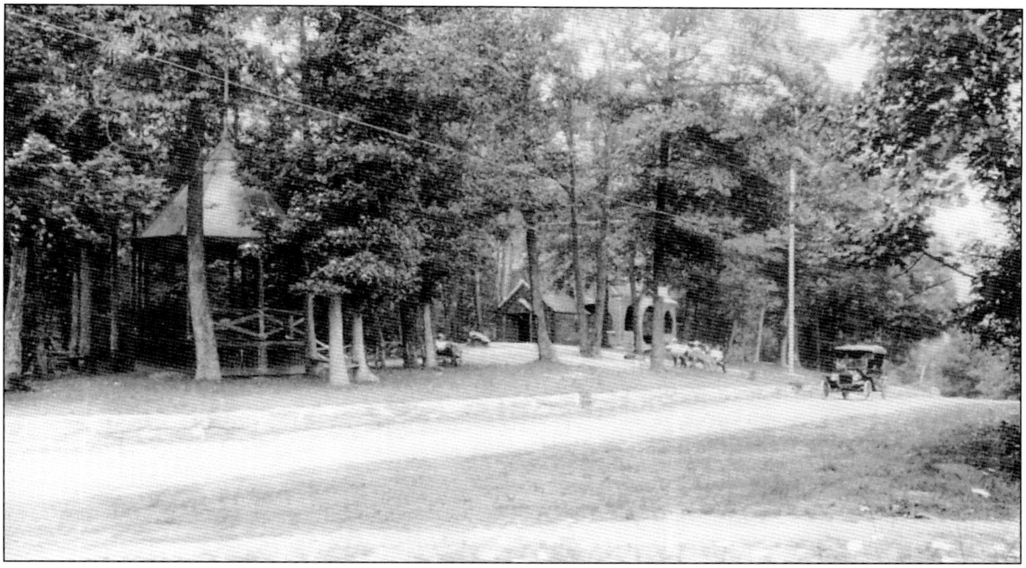

The park, pavilion, and pond have welcomed visitors since the early part of the century.

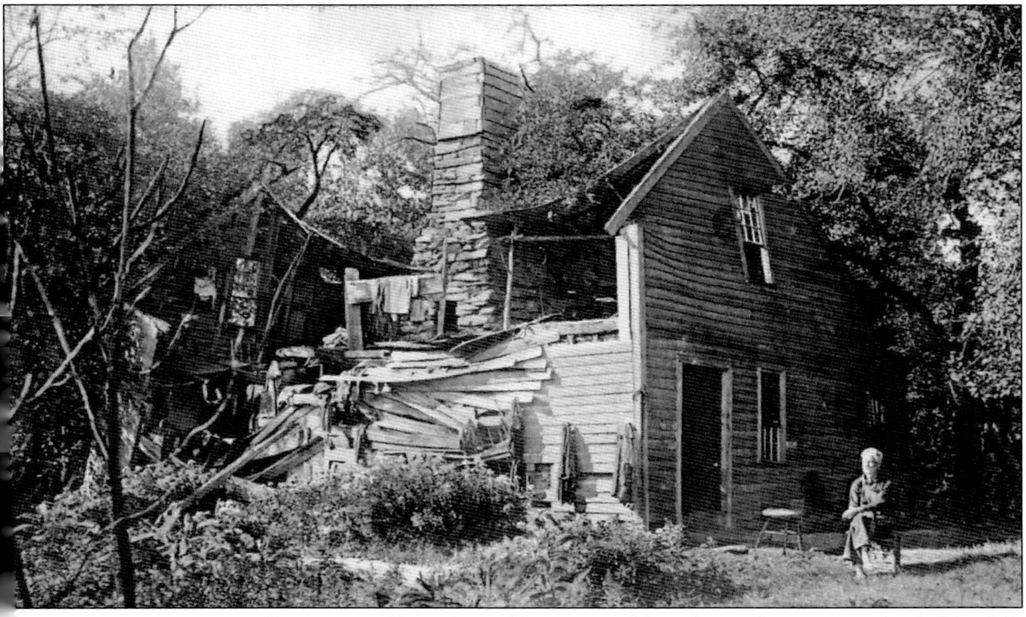

'he hermit George Washington Gilbert (possibly pictured here) is a figure in Ridgefield's folk .istory. The H.P. Bissell Co. published several postcards featuring scenes from the early 1900s.

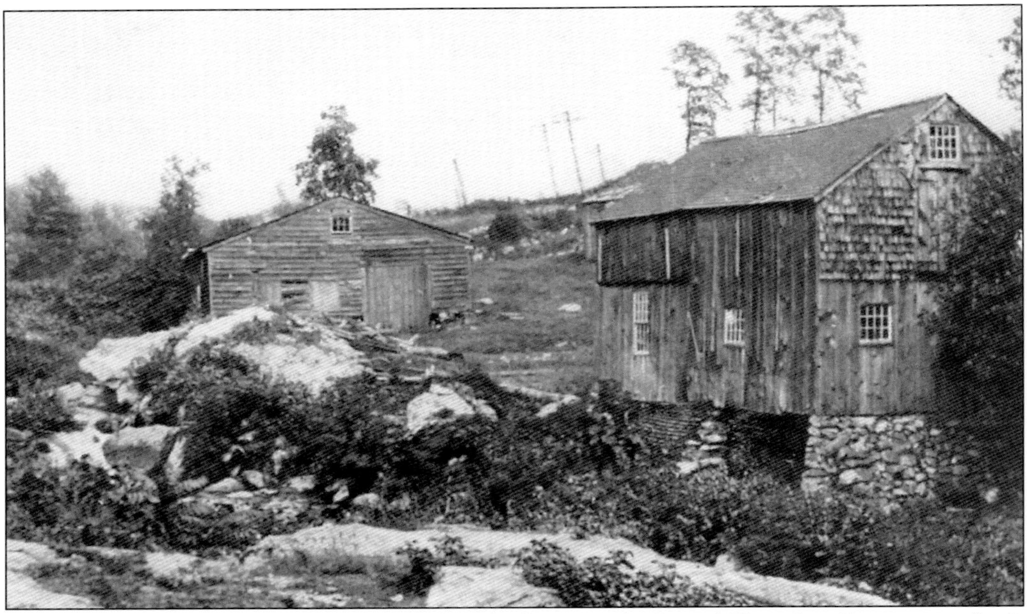

Weston has been a town for nearly two hundred years. The David Platt Axe Factory was built on the Aspetuck River.

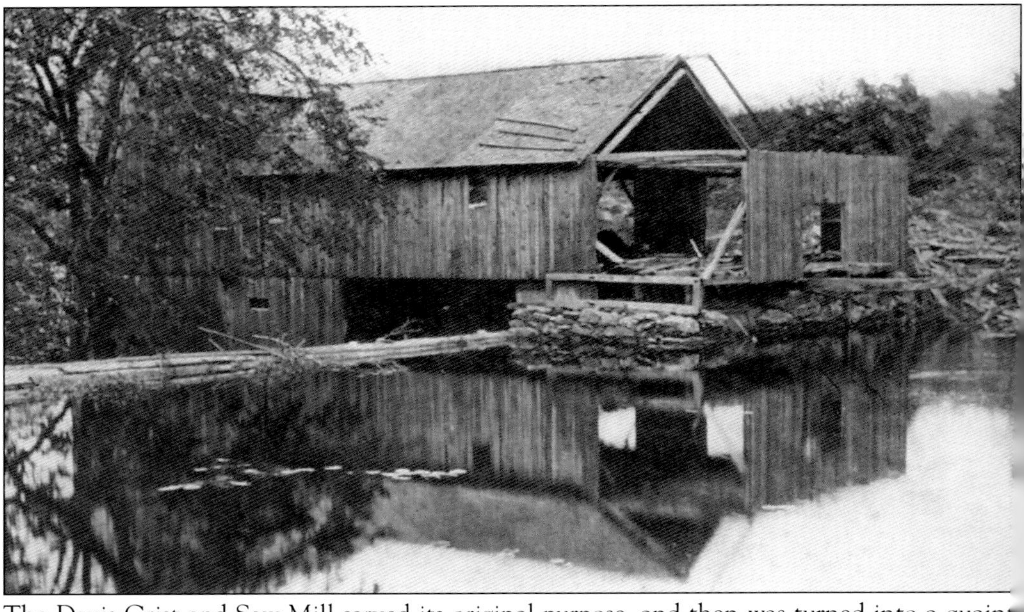

The Davis Grist and Saw Mill served its original purpose, and then was turned into a quaint attractive inn.

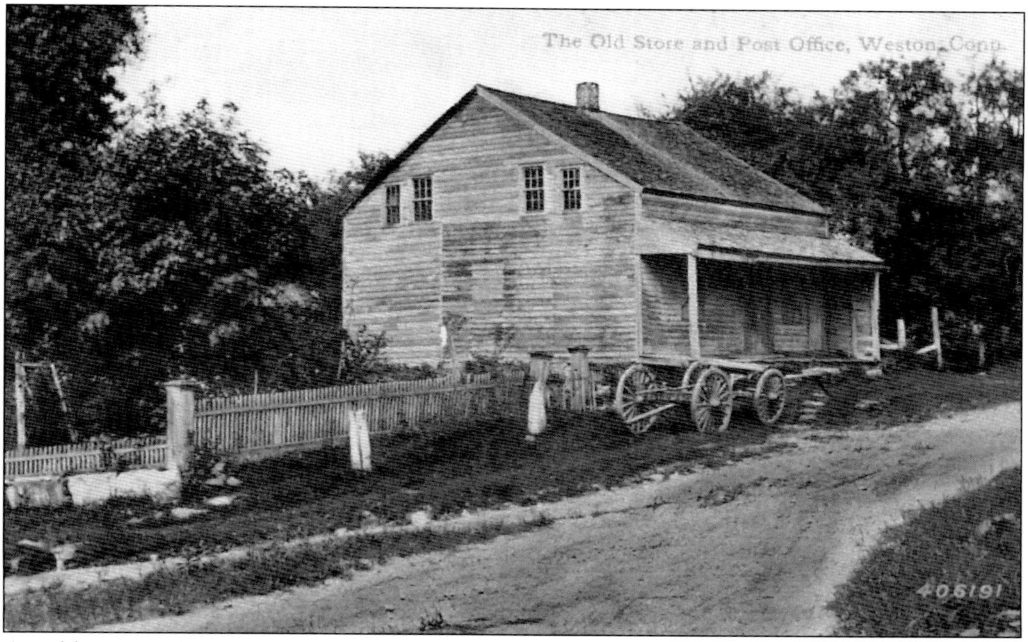

An old store and Weston's original post office have been restored in their original locations.

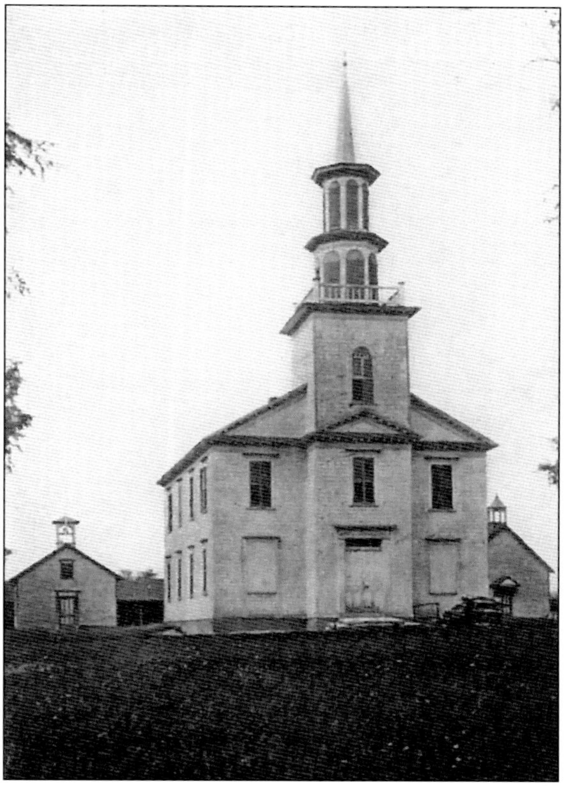

he Norfield Congregational
hurch continues life in the heart
f Weston; schools, shops, and
ther churches have joined it.

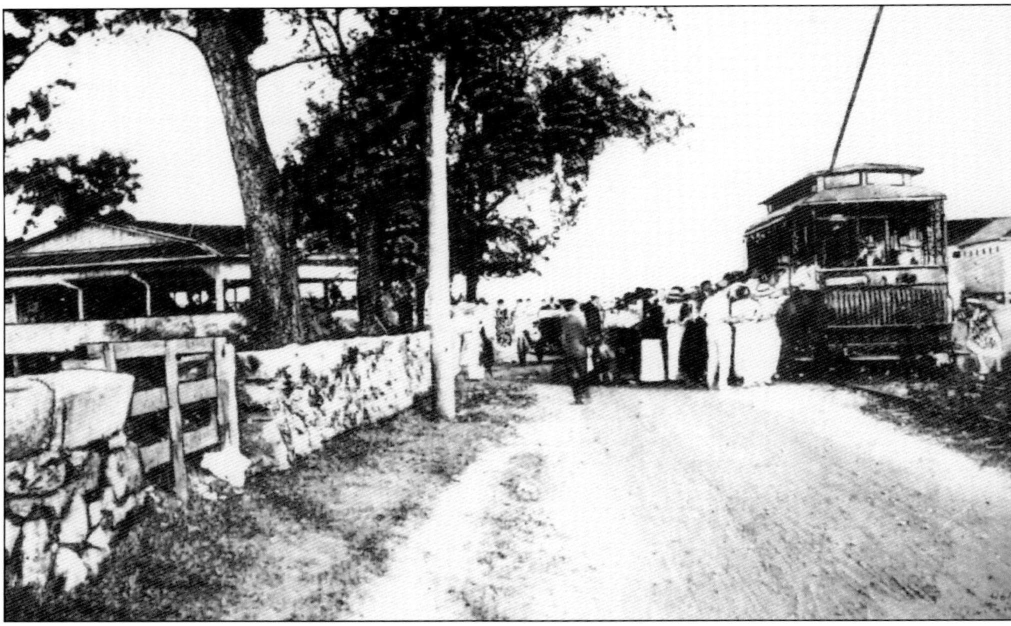

Westporters have enjoyed the advantages of their coastline on Long Island Sound. Here, passengers wait at a trolley terminal to go to Compo Beach.

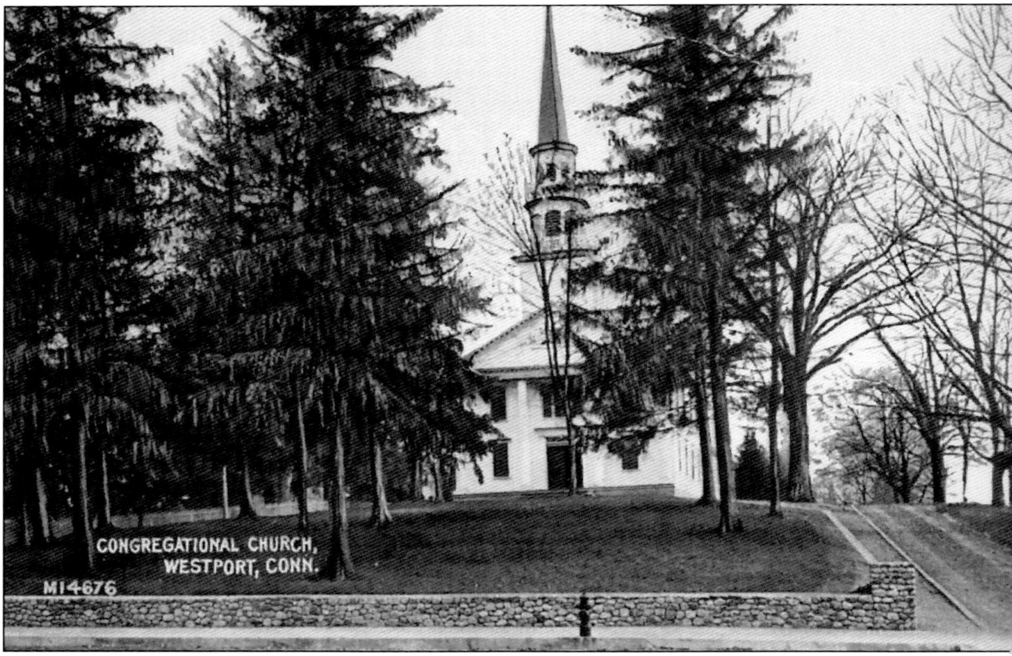

Westport, which grew from Weston, Fairfield, and Norwalk, also had its old church in the hear of the downtown district in 1835.

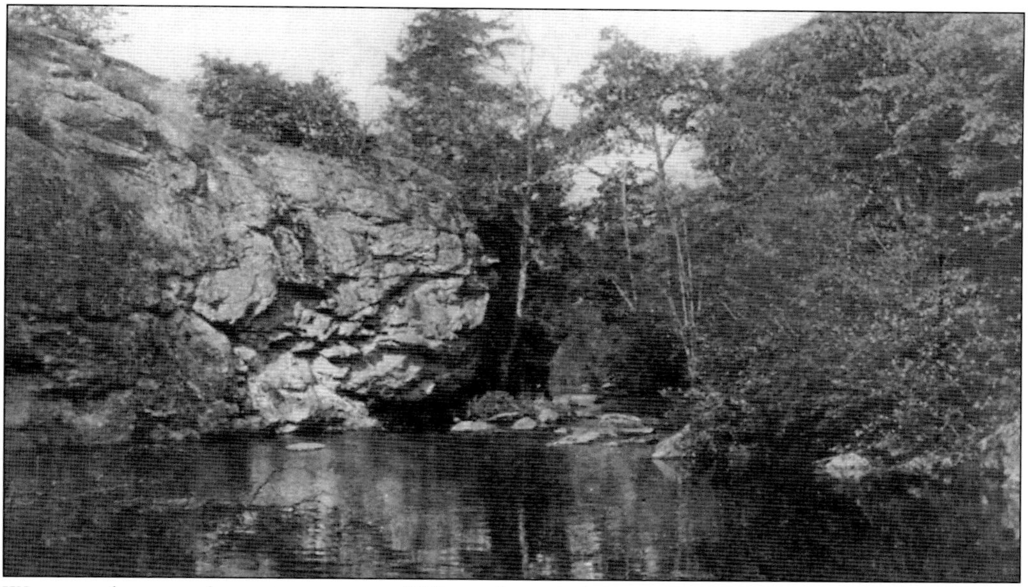

Water and a rugged terrain are part of Weston's appeal.

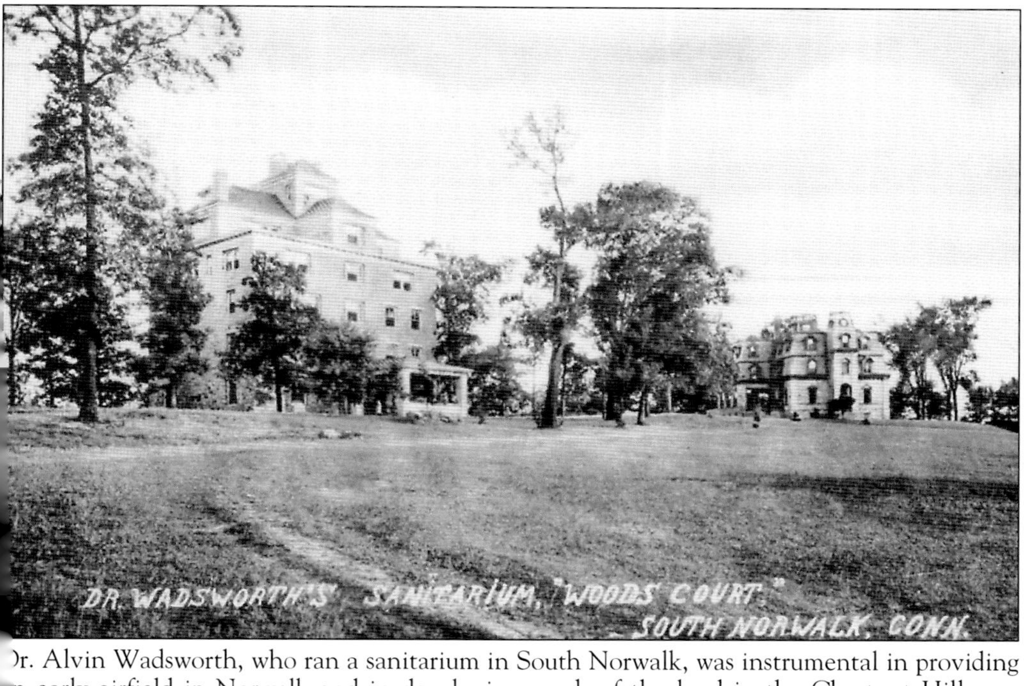

)r. Alvin Wadsworth, who ran a sanitarium in South Norwalk, was instrumental in providing n early airfield in Norwalk and in developing much of the land in the Chestnut Hill area f Wilton.

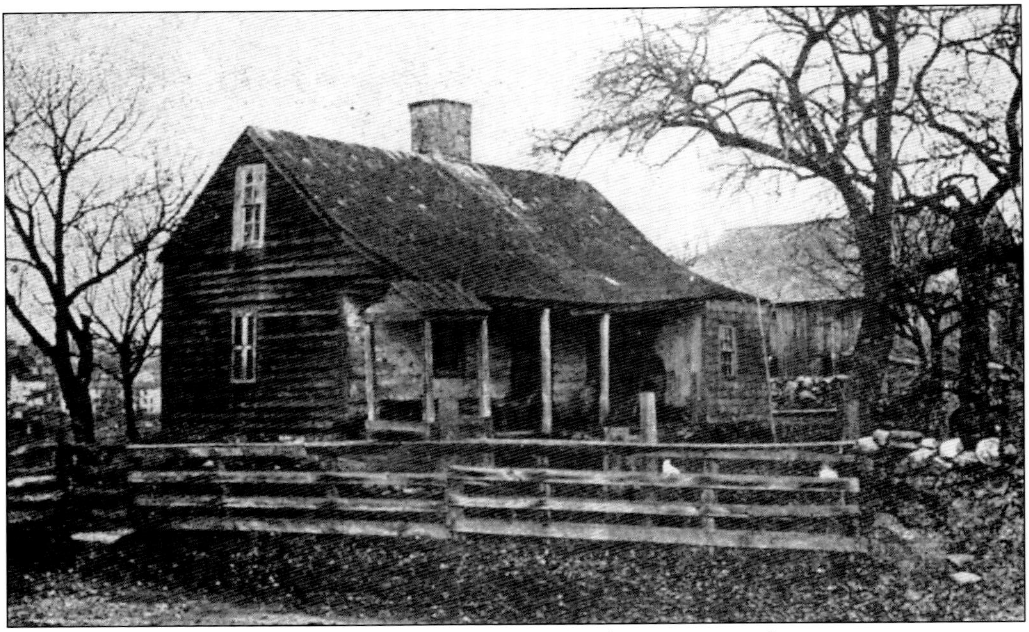

Norwalk's history has been gathered and conserved in books, pictures, and museum environments. The Yankee Doodle House, depicted in this card courtesy of D. Van Hoosear, Wilton historian, has been preserved with an old cemetery and the town house in Norwalk.

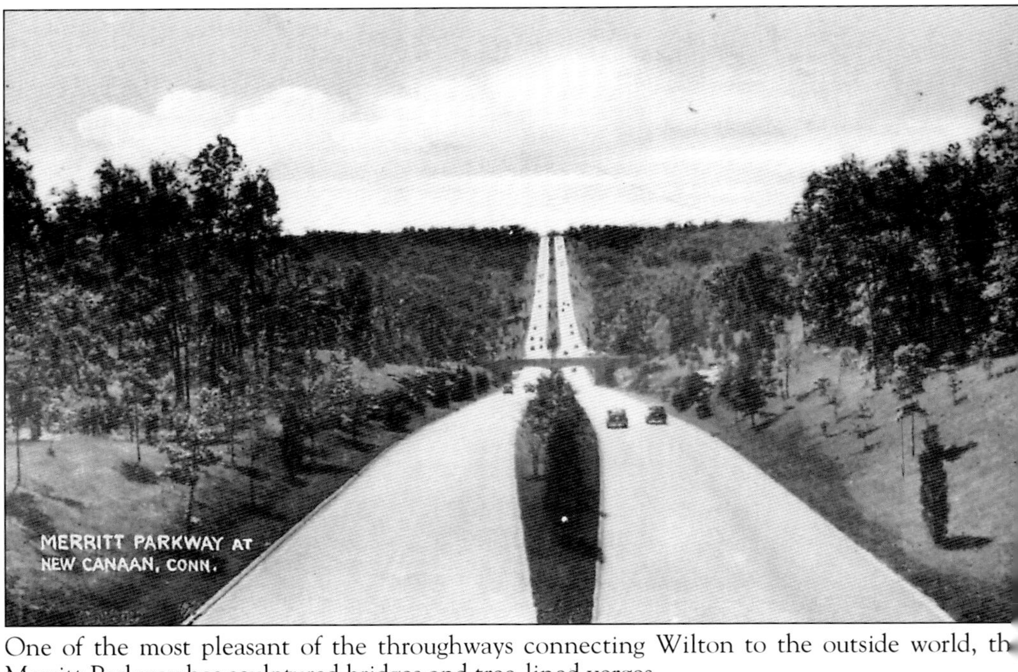

One of the most pleasant of the throughways connecting Wilton to the outside world, th Merritt Parkway has sculptured bridges and tree-lined verges.

References Relating to Postcard Publishing and Collecting

Allman, Dianne. *The Official Price Guide: Postcards.* 1st ed., New York: House of Collectibles (Random House), 1990.
Connecticut Postcard Club. *Charter Oak News.* Manchester, CT, 1996.
Corson, Walter E. and James Lewis Lowe, eds. *Publisher's Trademarks Identified.* Norwood, PA: James Lewis Lowe, 1993.
Dexter, Thomas. *The Dexter Press Story.* Upper Saddle River, NJ: Thomas A. Dexter, 1988.
Lengkeek, Deborah, ed. *Postcard Collector Annual: Commemorating 100 Years of the Postcard.* Iola, WI: Jones Publishing, 1993.

Acknowledgments

We wish to acknowledge and thank the many friends who have helped with encouragement, advice, loans, and gifts:

Harry Abbott
Edith Bader
Elizabeth Bader
Joan E. Bepler
Nancy Y. Brinley
Mary F. Channing
Rhoda Fischer
Margaret W. French
Nancy S. Johnson
Caroline Keeler
Amy H. Lindblom
Linnea Martin
Nancy K. Minnich
Ethel L. Nolan
Reverend Albert Ronander
Miriam N. Saunders
Anna Schlichting
The Wilton Historical Society (Marilyn Gould, director; Carol Russell, archivist)